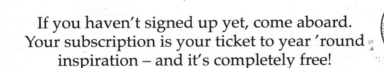

Check out our cooking videos on YouTube!

 Scan this code with your smartphone or tablet... it takes you right to our YouTube playlist of cooking videos for **5 Ingredients or Less**! While there, you can also view our entire collection of **Gooseberry Patch** cooking videos!

 If you spot this icon next to a recipe name, it means we created a video for it. You'll find it at **www.youtube.com/gooseberrypatchcom**.

Find Gooseberry Patch wherever you are!

www.gooseberrypatch.com

 Email

Call us toll-free at 1·800·854·6673

YOUR recipe could appear in our next cookbook!

Share your tried & true family favorites with us instantly at

www.gooseberrypatch.com

If you'd rather jot 'em down by hand, just mail this form to...
Gooseberry Patch • Cookbooks – Call for Recipes
2545 Farmers Dr., #380 • Columbus, OH 43235

If your recipe is selected for a book, you'll receive a FREE copy!

Please share only your original recipes or those that you have made your own over the years.

Recipe Name:

Number of Servings:

Any fond memories about this recipe? Special touches you like to add or handy shortcuts?

Ingredients (include specific measurements):

Instructions (continue on back if needed):

Special Code: **cookbookspage**

Over ➤

Extra space for recipe if needed:

Tell us about yourself...

Your complete contact information is needed so that we can send you your FREE cookbook, if your recipe is published. Phone numbers and email addresses are kept private and will only be used if we have questions about your recipe.

Name:

Address:

City: State: Zip:

Email:

Daytime Phone:

Thank you! Vickie & JoAnn

Gooseberry Patch
2545 Farmers Dr., #380
Columbus, OH 43235

www.gooseberrypatch.com

1•800•854•6673

Copyright 2013, Gooseberry Patch 978-1-62093-140-0
First Printing, November, 2013

Photo Edition is a major revision of *5 Ingredients or Less!*

U.S. to Metric Recipe Equivalents

Volume Measurements

1/4 teaspoon	1 mL
1/2 teaspoon	2 mL
1 teaspoon	5 mL
1 tablespoon = 3 teaspoons	15 mL
2 tablespoons = 1 fluid ounce	30 mL
1/4 cup	60 mL
1/3 cup	75 mL
1/2 cup = 4 fluid ounces	125 mL
1 cup = 8 fluid ounces	250 mL
2 cups = 1 pint =16 fluid ounces	500 mL
4 cups = 1 quart	1 L

Weights

1 ounce	30 g
4 ounces	120 g
8 ounces	225 g
16 ounces = 1 pound	450 g

Oven Temperatures

300° F	150° C
325° F	160° C
350° F	180° C
375° F	190° C
400° F	200° C
450° F	230° C

Baking Pan Sizes

Square

8x8x2 inches	2 L = 20x20x5 cm
9x9x2 inches	2.5 L = 23x23x5 cm

Rectangular

13x9x2 inches	3.5 L = 33x23x5 cm

Loaf

9x5x3 inches	2 L = 23x13x7 cm

Round

8x1-1/2 inches	1.2 L = 20x4 cm
9x1-1/2 inches	1.5 L = 23x4 cm

Contents

Dedication

To all of our friends who love
serving up simple and delicious
meals year 'round!

Appreciation

A big Gooseberry thanks to our friends
who sent their easiest, tried & true
recipes for every season.

Spring

The spring is here,
young and beautiful as ever.
- Henry Brooks Adams

spring

Cherry Tomato Poppers

Nancy Baker
Hagerstown, MD

Sprinkle these yummy tomatoes with fresh chopped parsley for a quick appetizer.

2 pts. cherry tomatoes
1 lb. bacon, crisply cooked and
   crumbled

1/2 c. mayonnaise
1/2 c. onion, minced
3 T. shredded mozzarella cheese

Hollow out cherry tomatoes; invert and drain on paper towels. Combine remaining ingredients; spoon into centers of tomatoes. Makes 2 to 3 dozen.

Blue Cheese-Onion Cheese Ball

Tricia Battersby
Woodhaven, MI

Serve with crackers, veggies or bagel chips.

8-oz. pkg. cream cheese,
   softened
4-oz. pkg. crumbled blue cheese

1/4 c. green olives, diced
1/4 c. onion, diced
3/4 c. chopped walnuts

Combine first 4 ingredients; mix well. Form into a round ball; roll in walnuts until covered. Serves 6 to 8.

Hang a swag of fresh flowers over doorways and garden gates to welcome springtime guests. Just secure stems to a raffia braid using florists' wire...so simple!

appetizers

Anytime Cheesy Biscuits

Naomi Cooper
Delaware, OH

So easy...you can whip them up in minutes!

2 c. biscuit baking mix
1/2 c. shredded Cheddar cheese
2/3 c. milk

1/4 c. margarine, melted
1/4 t. garlic powder

Combine first 3 ingredients together until a soft dough forms; beat vigorously for 30 seconds. Drop dough by rounded tablespoonfuls onto an ungreased baking sheet; bake at 450 degrees until golden, about 8 to 10 minutes. Whisk margarine and garlic powder together; spread over warm biscuits. Makes about 1-1/2 dozen.

Creamy Dill Dip

Donna Phair
Pittsfield, MA

Serve in a pumpernickel bread bowl and use bread cubes for dipping.

1 c. mayonnaise
1 c. sour cream
2 T. dill weed

2 T. Beau Monde seasoning
1 T. onion, minced

Combine ingredients; mix well. Cover and refrigerate for 2 to 3 hours before serving. Makes about 2 cups.

spring

Beef & Cheddar Quiche

Dianne Young
South Jordan, UT

So yummy topped with sour cream or even salsa!

3 eggs, beaten
1 c. whipping cream
1 c. shredded Cheddar cheese

1 c. ground beef, browned
9-inch pie crust

Mix eggs, cream, cheese and beef together; spread into pie crust. Bake at 450 degrees for 15 minutes; lower oven temperature to 350 degrees and continue baking for 15 minutes. Makes 8 servings.

Dress up pillar candles with eyelet lace, gingham ribbon or raffia bows...tuck in a fresh-picked blossom for the finishing touch.

appetizers

Thyme & Curry Dip

Patricia Carney
Lexington, NE

Serve with crunchy bread sticks or fresh veggies.

2 c. mayonnaise
4 T. chili sauce
4 t. tarragon vinegar

1/4 t. curry powder
1/4 t. dried thyme

Mix ingredients together; cover and chill for one hour. Makes 2 cups.

Sweet Onion Dip

Karen O'Brien
Midlothian, VA

No one ever believes this recipe is so easy...we love it with corn chips.

1-1/3 c. shredded sharp Cheddar
   cheese
1 c. mayonnaise

1 c. sweet onion, grated
1/8 t. hot pepper sauce

Mix ingredients together; spread in an ungreased 8"x8" baking pan.
Bake at 350 degrees for 20 minutes. Makes about 3 cups.

May your blessings outnumber the shamrocks that grow
And may trouble avoid you wherever you go.
- Irish Blessing

spring

Tuna Wrap-Ups

Sharon Hamill
Douglassville, PA

This is our family's variation on pigs in a blanket.
The kids usually fight over the last one!

6-oz. can tuna, drained
2 T. mayonnaise
salt and pepper to taste

8-oz. tube refrigerated crescent
rolls, separated
4 slices American cheese

Mix tuna, mayonnaise, salt and pepper together; set aside. Arrange crescents on an ungreased baking sheet; set aside. Fold cheese slices diagonally and break into 2 pieces; place one piece on each crescent. Spread one heaping tablespoon tuna mixture over cheese; roll up crescent roll-style. Bake at 375 degrees for 12 minutes. Makes 8.

Surprise a friend with the first blooms of Spring! Pick up some early annuals and leave them on her doorstep...a sweet reminder that Summer's right around the corner!

appetizers

Crab & Broccoli Rolls

Jane Moore
Haverford, PA

*Season with onion or garlic salt to taste or spice up with
a dash of hot pepper sauce!*

6-oz. can flaked crabmeat,
   drained
10-oz. pkg. frozen chopped
   broccoli, cooked, drained
   and cooled

1/4 c. mayonnaise
1/2 c. shredded Swiss cheese
8-oz. tube refrigerated crescent
   rolls, separated

Combine crab, broccoli, mayonnaise and cheese; spread about
2 tablespoonfuls on each crescent. Roll up crescent roll-style; arrange
on a lightly greased baking sheet. Bake at 375 degrees for 20 minutes.
Makes 8.

Super Salmon Dip

Beverly Boyd
Anchorage, AK

Serve with your favorite crackers or veggies.

8-oz. pkg. cream cheese,
   softened
1 T. milk

4-oz. can smoked salmon,
   chopped
4 green onions, minced

Blend cream cheese and milk until smooth and creamy; mix in salmon
and onions. Makes 1-1/2 cups.

Make a whimsical tablecloth out of a pretty floral sheet...just cut
down to size and add a ribbon border. For a no-sew
version, use iron-on binding for the edge.

spring

Orange Slushy

Connie Pritt
Coalton, WV

My reward for mowing the lawn...a cool and nutritious treat.

6-oz. can frozen orange juice
   concentrate
1/4 c. sugar

1 c. milk
1 t. vanilla extract
12 ice cubes

Place all ingredients in blender; blend to desired consistency. Serves 2.

Marshmallow Fruit Dip

Susan Young
Madison, AL

The kids forget fruit is good for them once they start dippin' away.

8-oz. pkg. cream cheese,
   softened
3 T. frozen orange juice
   concentrate

7-oz. jar marshmallow creme

Blend cream cheese and orange juice concentrate together until smooth; stir in marshmallow creme. Refrigerate until well chilled. Makes about 2 cups.

Fresh-cut blooms look so pretty in Grandma's teapot. Look for tulips, daffodils and white daisies to brighten up the buffet or kitchen table.

appetizers

Strawberry-Watermelon Slush

Sandy Benham
Sanborn, NY

*A luscious combination of fresh summer fruit. Slip a plump
strawberry onto a drinking straw for a fun garnish.*

1 pt. strawberries, hulled and
   halved
2 c. watermelon, seeded and
   cubed

1/3 c. sugar
1/3 c. lemon juice
2 c. ice cubes

Combine strawberries, watermelon, sugar and lemon juice in a
blender. Blend until smooth. Gradually add ice and continue to blend.
Serve immediately. Makes 5 to 6 servings.

Add whimsy to a plain wooden frame with upholstery tacks. They
come in all shapes and sizes and are easily applied with a tap
from a rubber mallet. Use one in each corner or create
a row all around the frame.

spring

Easy Gumbo Meatballs

Brenda Flowers
Olney, IL

*After baking, keep these warm in the slow cooker...they're
a potluck favorite!*

2 lbs. ground beef
4 slices bread, crumbled
3/4 c. evaporated milk

10-3/4 oz. can chicken
   gumbo soup
10-1/2 oz. can French onion
   soup

Combine first 3 ingredients together; form into one-inch balls. Arrange
in an ungreased 13"x9" baking pan; pour soups on top. Bake at
350 degrees for 1-1/2 hours. Serves 6.

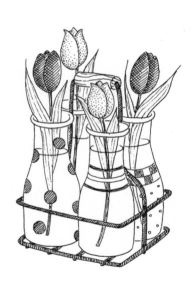

Vintage glass milk bottles and vases can be dressed up
with paint...many craft varieties are made just for glass.
Paint festive polka dots, stripes in old-fashioned
colors or a whimsical checkerboard.

Reuben Appetizers

Carol Hickman
Kingsport, TN

Put it together in minutes and they'll be gone in seconds.

1 loaf sliced party rye
1/2 c. Thousand Island salad
  dressing
1/2 lb. sliced corned beef

14-oz. can sauerkraut, drained
6-oz. pkg. shredded Swiss
  cheese

Spread bread with dressing; set aside. Slice corned beef to fit bread; place 2 slices on each bread slice. Top with one to 2 teaspoons sauerkraut; sprinkle with cheese. Arrange on an ungreased baking sheet; bake at 350 degrees for 10 minutes or until cheese melts. Serves 12.

Saucy Sausages

Lynn Teska
Palatine, IL

So easy and oh-so tasty!

1-lb. pkg. cooked Polish
  sausage, sliced

21-oz. can cherry pie filling

Arrange sausage slices in an ungreased 9"x9" baking pan; spread cherry pie filling on top. Bake at 350 degrees for 45 minutes. Arrange on a serving platter; serve with party toothpicks. Serves 4.

Brightly colored stepping
stones add cheer to
still-sleeping flower beds...
they'll blend right in when
the flowers come up!

spring

Texas Caviar

Kathy Wood
La Crescenta, CA

Serve this dip with multi-colored tortilla chips.

15-oz. can black beans, rinsed
    and drained
15-oz. can black-eyed peas,
    rinsed and drained

15-1/4 oz. can corn, drained
16-oz. jar salsa

Stir ingredients together; pour into an airtight container. Refrigerate several hours before serving. Serves 10.

Sizzling Salsa Dip

Debbie Sundermeier
Brunswick, OH

If you like it hot, this is the dip for you...try it once and you'll be addicted.

1 lb. hot Italian ground sausage,
    browned
16-oz. jar hot salsa

16-oz. pkg. pasteurized process
    mild Mexican cheese spread,
    cubed

Combine ingredients in a slow cooker; heat on low setting until cheese melts, stirring frequently. Makes about 3-1/2 cups.

Keep your blooms standing tall
in a picnic centerpiece.
Slip stems into clear drinking
straws and they'll keep
their heads up all day!

appetizers

Pepperoni Pizza Bites

Nancy Kremkus
Ann Arbor, MI

So fun to make with the kids!

11.3-oz. tube refrigerated dinner
   rolls
15-oz. can pizza sauce

4-oz. pkg. sliced pepperoni
1-1/2 c. shredded mozzarella
   cheese

Arrange dinner rolls about 3 inches apart on a lightly greased baking
sheet; flatten each roll into a 2-inch circle. Pinch edges to make a
slight rim; spoon pizza sauce into each center. Add a few pepperoni
slices; sprinkle with cheese. Bake according to dinner roll package
directions. Makes 8.

*H*osting a get-together to celebrate Spring? Make clever
invitations using pressed flowers or stamps
from the first green leaves.

spring

Cheesy Chicken & Noodle Soup

Christi Perry
Denton, TX

Spice it up...top with shredded Pepper Jack cheese.

2 to 3 c. chicken, cooked and
    shredded
10-3/4 oz. can Cheddar cheese
    soup
4 to 6 c. chicken broth

8-oz. pkg. fine egg noodles
1 c. milk
Optional: shredded Cheddar
    cheese

Combine all ingredients except cheese in a large stockpot; bring to a
boil over medium heat. Reduce heat; simmer until noodles are soft.
Spoon into bowls; sprinkle with cheese, if desired. Serves 6 to 8.

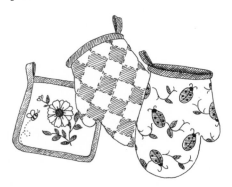

Bits of Sunshine Biscuits

Donna Bowles
Plant City, FL

*Served for breakfast alongside scrambled eggs or
with a bowl of soup, they'll be a hit.*

1 c. margarine, melted
8-oz. pkg. shredded sharp
    Cheddar cheese

1 c. sour cream
2 c. self-rising flour

Combine margarine and cheese; set aside to cool for 2 minutes. Add
sour cream; stir in flour. Fill greased mini muffin tins 2/3 full; bake at
350 degrees for 20 to 25 minutes. Makes about 4 dozen.

soups & breads

Sunday Meeting Tomato Soup

Gretchen Ham
Pine City, NY

Fresh basil really makes this soup special. It's often requested at our church's Sunday soup & sandwich lunches after the services.

1/2 c. butter, sliced
1 c. fresh basil, chopped
2 28-oz. cans crushed tomatoes
2 cloves garlic, minced

1 qt. half-and-half
salt and pepper to taste
Garnish: croutons, shredded
    Parmesan cheese

In a large saucepan, melt butter over medium heat. Add basil; sauté for 2 minutes. Add tomatoes with juice and garlic. Reduce heat and simmer for 20 minutes. Remove from heat; let cool slightly. Working in batches, transfer tomato mixture to a blender and purée. Transfer back into saucepan and add half-and-half, mixing well. Reheat soup over medium-low heat; add salt and pepper to taste. Serve topped with croutons and shredded Parmesan cheese. Makes 10 servings.

Braided homespun rugs are at home in any room but they look especially cozy in front of the fireplace, the sink or the stove. Look for nostalgic rag rugs at flea markets and antique shops.

Beefy Taco Soup

Erin McRae
Beaverton, OR

Top each bowl with corn chips, sour cream and
a sprinkling of shredded cheese.

1 lb. ground beef, browned
14.5-oz. can stewed tomatoes
15-oz. can kidney beans, rinsed
    and drained

1-1/4 oz. pkg. taco seasoning
    mix
8-oz. can tomato sauce

Stir ingredients together; pour into a slow cooker. Heat on low setting
for 6 to 8 hours; stir occasionally. Add water to thin consistency as
desired. Makes 4 to 6 servings.

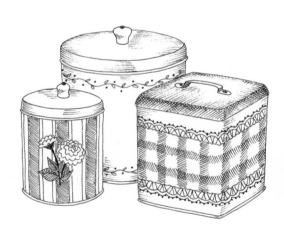

Put together a set of canisters for a blushing bride-to-be.
Pick up a mismatched set in retro colors and
toss in a few tried & true recipes as well.

soups & breads

Too-Simple Tortilla Soup

Paulette Cunningham
Lompoc, CA

Top with a couple of slices of avocado and a dollop of sour cream.

3 5-oz. cans chicken
2 14-1/2 oz. cans chicken broth
2 15-oz. cans white hominy
16-oz. jar picante sauce
1 T. cumin

Combine ingredients together in a stockpot; bring to a boil. Reduce heat and warm through. Makes 6 to 8 servings.

White Bean Chicken Chili

Kristie Matry
Ada, MI

Make it a meal...serve with crusty rolls and a fresh salad.

48-oz. jar Great Northern beans
4 boneless, skinless chicken
   breasts, cooked
16-oz. jar salsa
8-oz. pkg. shredded Monterey
   Jack cheese
8-oz. pkg. jalapeño cheese,
   cubed

Add ingredients to a stockpot; heat over low heat until cheeses melt. Stir in up to one cup water for desired consistency; heat until warmed through. Serves 4 to 6.

The world's favorite season is Spring.
All things seem possible in May.
- Edwin Way Teale

spring

Parmesan-Garlic Biscuits

Jo Ann

These upside-down biscuits are a hit with any Italian dish!

3 T. butter, melted
1/4 t. celery seed
2 cloves garlic, minced

12-oz. tube refrigerated biscuits
2 T. grated Parmesan cheese

Coat bottom of a 9" pie pan with butter; add celery seed and garlic. Slice each biscuit into quarters; arrange on top of butter mixture. Sprinkle with Parmesan cheese; bake at 425 degrees for 12 to 15 minutes. Invert onto a serving plate to serve. Makes 8 servings.

Zesty Pizza Soup

Kim Stokes
Malden, MO

Layer a slice of French bread with a slice of mozzarella cheese into each bowl, then spoon soup on top.

3 onions, diced
1 tomato, chopped
2 potatoes, peeled and cubed

dried oregano and garlic salt
to taste
2 c. water

Combine all ingredients except water together in a large saucepan; stir in water and heat until vegetables are tender. Serves 2.

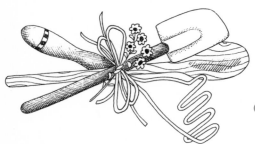

Add garlic braids to kitchen décor...hang them next to the door or along with copper pots on a wrought iron rack.

Pot O' Gold

Julie Wise
Delaware, OH

At Girl Scout camp, we cook this over an open fire...just as good when made on the stovetop.

1 lb. ground beef
1 onion, chopped
3 10-3/4 oz. cans tomato soup

12-oz. tube refrigerated biscuits
8-oz. pkg. Cheddar cheese, cubed

Brown ground beef with onion; drain. Add to a stockpot; pour in soup and 3 soup cans water. Bring to a boil over medium heat; reduce until simmering. Divide biscuits; insert one cube cheese into the center of each biscuit. Spoon biscuits into soup; cover and simmer for 20 minutes. Makes 8 servings.

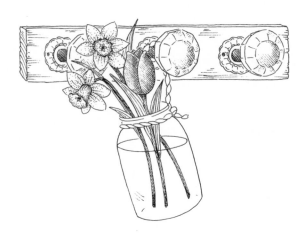

Looking for a way to display those vintage glass doorknobs? Create a whimsical peg board in an afternoon...just screw them into a weathered piece of wood using vintage-style hardware, attach metal picture hangers to the back and mount to a wall. Hang baskets, fresh spring blooms or even a straw hat!

spring

Sour Cream Mini Biscuits

Jeanne Barringer
Edgewater, FL

Once you start snacking on these, it's hard to stop!

1 c. butter, softened   2 c. self-rising flour
1 c. sour cream

Blend butter and sour cream together until fluffy; gradually mix in flour. Drop by teaspoonfuls into greased mini muffin tins; bake at 450 degrees for 10 to 12 minutes. Makes 4 dozen.

Search for vintage egg cups at flea markets and antique shops...so pretty on the breakfast table or lined up on the windowsill. These dainty cups were made of everything from hobnail milk glass, porcelain to even sterling silver!

soups & breads

Old-Fashioned Salmon Soup

Phyllis Peters
Three Rivers, MI

During the Depression, money was tight and families found salmon was a way to stretch the grocery budget. This soup is delicious with soda crackers and it's a filling comfort food...add more milk to stretch the soup even further.

14-3/4 oz. can salmon, mashed
1 T. butter

3 c. milk
salt and pepper to taste

Combine all ingredients in a saucepan; heat until hot without boiling. Serves 2.

Creamy Crab Stew

Helen VonWaldner
Savannah, GA

Serve with cheese crackers or crunchy sourdough bread.

1 lb. crabmeat, cooked
10-3/4 oz. can cream of
   celery soup

10-3/4 oz. can cream of
   chicken soup

Mix all ingredients together; add one soup can water. Mix well and heat thoroughly without boiling. Makes 4 to 6 servings.

Surprise a new neighbor with a stack of soup bowls wrapped up in a tea towel along with a favorite soup recipe...don't forget the crackers!

spring

Hidden Pear Salad

Cindy Coffman
Lewisberry, PA

A classic fruity gelatin salad...so refreshing!

16-oz. can pears, drained and
    juice reserved
3-oz. pkg. lime gelatin mix
3-oz. pkg. cream cheese,
    softened

1/4 t. lemon juice
1.3-oz. pkg. whipped topping
    mix

Pour pear juice into a saucepan; bring to a boil over medium heat. Remove from heat; stir in gelatin until dissolved. Set aside to cool to room temperature. Purée pears in a blender; set aside. Blend cream cheese and lemon juice until light and fluffy; mix in pears and set aside. Prepare whipped topping according to package directions; fold into pear mixture. Add cooled gelatin; pour into a mold and chill overnight. Makes 6 to 8 servings.

For a sparkly centerpiece, brush fresh fruit and greenery with watered-down glue and then sprinkle with superfine glitter.

Salads & Sides

Spicy Peach Salad

Sherri Hunt
Garland, TX

A wonderfully rich side dish made from just 4 ingredients.

3-oz. pkg. orange gelatin mix
29-oz. can whole spiced
   peaches, chopped and juice
   reserved

1/2 c. chopped pecans
8-oz. pkg. chopped dates

Prepare orange gelatin according to package directions, substituting one cup peach juice for the water; chill until slightly thickened. Fold in peaches, pecans and dates; pour into a mold or serving bowl. Chill until set. Serves 4.

5-Cup Salad

Becky Willis
Greenwood, IN

Light and fluffy!

1 c. pineapple tidbits, drained
1 c. mini marshmallows
1 c. flaked coconut

1 c. mandarin oranges, drained
1 c. sour cream

Gently stir ingredients together in a serving bowl; cover and chill until serving. Makes 6 servings.

Hang a sturdy wooden spoon sideways on a wall...add 3 cup hooks for a handy kitchen pegboard.

spring

Crunchy Corn Chip Salad

Linda Bethel
Shidler, OK

Double or triple the recipe for large gatherings.

11-oz. can sweet corn and diced
   peppers, drained
1/3 c. green pepper, minced

1/4 c. green onion, chopped
10-oz. pkg. corn chips
8-oz. bottle ranch salad dressing

Combine corn, green pepper and onion together in a large serving bowl; refrigerate until ready to serve. Add corn chips and enough ranch dressing to moisten. Serve immediately. Makes 6 servings.

Use Grandma's pressed glass cake stand to make a centerpiece of pillar candles. Stack the tallest in the center and shorter ones toward the outside...tuck in seasonal greenery and fresh flowers to add a warm glow to dinner.

Pea & Peanut Salad

*Ginger Bennett
Royal Oak, MI*

Yummy when made with honey-roasted peanuts too.

10-oz. pkg. frozen peas, thawed
    and drained
1 c. Spanish peanuts

1/2 c. sour cream
1/2 c. mayonnaise
1 T. sugar

Gently stir ingredients together in a serving bowl; cover and chill until serving. Serves 4.

Marinated Broccoli Salad

*Beverly Brown
Bowie, MD*

So easy...mix in the bag!

2 bunches broccoli flowerets,
    chopped
1 t. dill weed

1/2 c. oil
1/2 c. red wine vinegar
2 cloves garlic, minced

Place ingredients in a gallon plastic zipping bag; close and shake well. Refrigerate overnight, shaking occasionally; serve chilled. Serves 6.

When spring days warm up, plan a picnic with friends & family. Ask everyone to bring a dish and a blanket too!

spring

Maple-Glazed Carrots

Andrea Heyart
Aubrey, TX

*These sweet and savory carrots are a perfect addition to
your family's table or a fun potluck!*

4-1/2 c. water
4 lbs. carrots, peeled and sliced
10 T. butter, divided
6 T. brown sugar, packed and
    divided

1-1/2 t. salt
6 T. maple syrup
Garnish: snipped fresh chives

Bring water to a boil in a large saucepan over medium-high heat.
Add carrots, 4 tablespoons butter, 3 tablespoons brown sugar and
salt. Reduce heat to medium-low. Cover and simmer just until carrots
are tender when pierced with a fork, about 10 minutes. Drain and
set aside. Melt remaining butter in a large skillet over medium-high
heat. Add maple syrup and remaining brown sugar; cook and stir until
sugar has dissolved. Reduce heat to medium-low. Add carrots to syrup
mixture and toss gently. Cook for 5 minutes, or until carrots are evenly
coated and mixture is bubbly. Sprinkle with chives just before serving.
Serves 10.

Start cool weather veggies like lettuce and spinach indoors in
old wooden drawers and get a jump start on the garden! Just line
with plastic, add gravel for drainage and plant away. They
can go directly outside once the days warm up.

Citrus Apple Sweet Potatoes

Carolyn Kent
Evant, TX

Our family loves these potatoes alongside a slice of ham.

6 sweet potatoes, peeled, boiled
   and mashed
2 c. applesauce

1/2 c. brown sugar, packed
4 T. butter
1/2 c. orange juice

Mix ingredients together; place in a lightly buttered 2-quart casserole dish. Bake at 350 degrees for 40 minutes. Serves 8 to 10.

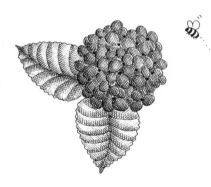

Grandma's Buttery Mashed Potatoes

J.J. Presley
Portland, TX

Grandma used to make these mashed potatoes every Sunday for lunch no matter what the main course was. I can still taste them to this day!

6 to 8 potatoes, peeled and
   cubed
1/2 c. butter, softened
1 c. evaporated milk

salt and pepper to taste
Garnish: additional butter,
   fresh chives

Cover potatoes with water in a large saucepan; bring to a boil over medium-high heat. Cook until tender, about 15 minutes; drain. Add remaining ingredients. Beat with an electric mixer on medium speed until blended and creamy. Garnish as desired. Serves 8 to 12.

Baked Chiles Rellenos

*Jean Edwards
Citrus Heights, CA*

This Mexican standard is so easy to put together.

7-oz. can whole green chiles
1/2 lb. sharp Cheddar cheese
2 eggs

1/2 c. all-purpose flour
1-1/2 c. milk

Slice chiles down the center; arrange in a lightly buttered
13"x9" baking pan and set aside. Slice cheese to fit inside chiles;
place in chiles. Whisk egg, flour and milk together; pour over
chiles. Bake at 350 degrees for 45 to 50 minutes. Serves 4.

Green Chile Rice

*Debbie Wilson
Weatherford, TX*

Sprinkle with diced jalapeño peppers for an extra kick!

3 c. prepared rice
12-oz. pkg. shredded mozzarella
   cheese

2 c. sour cream
4-oz. can diced green chiles

Combine ingredients; pour into an ungreased 1-1/2 quart casserole
dish. Mix well; bake at 400 degrees until bubbly, about 20 minutes.
Makes 6 servings.

What a thoughtful
housewarming gift! Give neighbors
a new mailbox including the house
number, address labels, stationery
and stamps. Don't forget to include
some fun pens too.

Taco Salad Dressing

Kay Twining
Tampa, FL

This dressing is great on taco salad but don't be afraid to try it on any salad...keep it in a squeeze bottle in the fridge!

1/2 c. catsup
1 c. oil
3/4 c. sugar

1/4 c. vinegar
1 T. hot pepper sauce

Whisk ingredients together; cover and refrigerate until serving. Makes about 2-1/2 cups.

Corn for a Crowd

Bonnie Huckabee
San Angelo, TX

A real crowd pleaser!

5-lb. bag frozen corn
2 8-oz. pkgs. cream cheese,
   cubed and softened

1/2 c. sweetened condensed
   milk

Prepare corn according to package directions; stir in cream cheese until melted. Drizzle milk on top; mix well. Serves 25.

spring

Sweet & Spicy Chicken

Joan Sumner
Callao, VA

With 4 simple ingredients, this marinated chicken
is great for springtime cookouts.

1/2 c. orange juice
1/4 c. honey
1-oz. pkg. Italian salad
    dressing mix

6 boneless, skinless chicken
    breasts

Mix first 3 ingredients together; add chicken breasts. Marinate for
one hour, turning to coat both sides. Grill or broil until juices run clear
when pierced with a fork. Makes 6 servings.

Creamy Apricot Chicken

Tami Hoffman
Litchfield, NH

Serve over a bed of white rice.

8-oz. jar Russian salad dressing
12-oz. jar apricot preserves

1 to 2 lbs. boneless, skinless
    chicken breasts

Combine salad dressing and preserves together; set aside. Arrange
chicken in a slow cooker; pour dressing mixture on top. Heat on low
setting for 6 to 8 hours. Makes 4 to 6 servings.

Sweet Spring, full of sweet days and roses.
    - George Herbert

mains

Oven-Baked Chicken Fingers

Kathy Wood
La Crescenta, CA

Serve with ranch dressing or barbecue sauce for dipping.

1 c. Italian bread crumbs
2 T. grated Parmesan cheese
1 clove garlic, minced

1/4 c. oil
6 boneless, skinless chicken
    breasts

Shake bread crumbs and cheese together in plastic zipping bag; set aside. Combine garlic and oil in a small bowl; set aside. Flatten chicken to 1/2-inch thickness; cut into one-inch wide strips. Dip strips in oil mixture; coat with crumb mixture. Arrange on a greased baking sheet; bake at 350 degrees for 20 minutes, turning after 10 minutes. Serves 6.

Vintage glass salt and pepper shakers can be put to new use as tiny single bud vases...wire a mismatched pair together and hang from a pegboard or on the back of guests' chairs.

Easy Slow-Cooker Steak

Ashley Whitehead
Sidney, TX

Like lots of gravy? Use 2 packages of soup mix and 2 cans of soup.

2 to 2-1/2 lb. round steak
1-1/2 oz. pkg. onion soup mix

10-3/4 oz. can cream of
mushroom soup

Slice steak into 5 serving-size pieces; place in a slow cooker. Add soup mix, 1/4 cup water and soup; cover and cook on low for 6 to 8 hours. Makes 5 servings.

A pretty table centerpiece for a twilight baby shower...float tea lights in glass dessert dishes. Group 3 or 4 dishes per table and light for a magical night.

mains

Saucy Pork Chops

Cindy McCormick
Bakersfield, CA

This saucy bake works well with chicken too!

2 10-3/4 oz. cans cream of
   chicken soup
1/2 c. catsup

6 t. Worcestershire sauce
4 to 6 pork chops
2-1/2 c. prepared rice

Mix soup, catsup and Worcestershire sauce together; set aside. Arrange pork chops in an ungreased 13"x9" baking pan; pour soup mixture over the top. Cover and bake for one hour at 350 degrees. Serve each pork chop on a serving of rice; spoon remaining sauce on top. Makes 4 to 6 servings.

Crispy Pork Cutlets

Patricia Roisum
Marshall, WI

Crispy and tender, serve these cutlets with mashed potatoes.

2 eggs
2 T. mustard
2 lbs. pork cutlets

1 c. instant mashed potato
   flakes
3 T. oil

Blend eggs and mustard together in a shallow pie pan; set aside. Dip pork cutlets in egg mixture; coat with potato flakes. Heat oil in a skillet; add pork, heating on both sides until done. Serves 4 to 6.

spring

Toasted Ravioli

Fran Hynek
Bellevue, NE

Dip in warmed pizza sauce...scrumptious!

25-oz. pkg. frozen ravioli
1 c. bread crumbs
1/4 c. grated Parmesan cheese

1 egg, beaten
1/4 c. milk

Prepare ravioli according to package directions; drain. Combine bread crumbs and Parmesan cheese together in a pie pan; set aside. Whisk egg and milk together; set aside. Dip ravioli in egg mixture; coat with bread crumb mixture. Sauté in a skillet until golden, adding one tablespoon olive oil if necessary; drain. Serves 4.

Coordinate a garden gift in a new flower pot...paint the pot to match the gloves then tuck in seed packets and a new trowel.

mains

Pizza Mac & Cheese

Jesse Ireland
St. Augustine, FL

My grandmother always made this recipe for my sister and me when we visited...it was a treat we looked forward to all year long.

7-1/4 oz. pkg. macaroni & cheese
2 eggs, beaten

16-oz. jar pizza sauce
4-oz. pkg. sliced pepperoni
1 c. shredded mozzarella cheese

Prepare macaroni and cheese according to package directions; remove from heat. Add eggs; mix well. Pour into a greased 13"x9" baking pan; bake at 375 degrees for 10 minutes. Spread with pizza sauce; layer pepperoni and mozzarella cheese on top. Return to oven until cheese melts, about 10 minutes. Makes 8 servings.

Poppy's Onion Pizza

Lisa Arning
Garden City, NY

My dad became a wonderful cook when he retired...he passed this traditional Italian recipe on to me.

3 T. olive oil, divided
10-inch refrigerated pizza crust
2 onions, diced

garlic powder to taste
paprika to taste
Optional: salt and pepper to taste

Lightly coat pizza pan with one tablespoon olive oil; place pizza dough into pan. Coat dough with one tablespoon olive oil; set aside. Sauté onions in remaining olive oil until golden; spread evenly over the dough, lightly pressing down. Sprinkle with garlic powder and paprika; add salt and pepper, if desired. Bake at 425 degrees until golden, about 20 minutes. Makes 8 servings.

Zesty Picante Chicken

Sonya Collett
Sioux City, IA

We like to double the recipe and just roll up the leftovers in tortillas...tomorrow's dinner is ready!

4 boneless, skinless chicken
  breasts
16-oz. jar picante sauce
15-1/2 oz. can black beans,
  drained and rinsed

4 slices American cheese
2-1/4 c. prepared rice

Place chicken in the bottom of a slow cooker; add picante sauce. Spread black beans over the top; heat on low setting for 6 to 8 hours or until juices run clear when chicken is pierced with a fork. Top with cheese slices; cover and heat until melted. Spoon over rice to serve. Serves 4.

For a garden party, arrange flowers or vegetable bouquets in produce baskets or miniature watering cans. Insert seed packets attached to bamboo skewers into the arrangements or use them to identify the dishes served.

Cheesy Fiesta Bake

Brittany Trotter-McDowell
Ellsinore, MO

Top with shredded lettuce, chopped tomatoes, sliced olives and sour cream after baking.

2 lbs. ground beef, browned
1-1/4 oz. pkg. taco seasoning
   mix
2 8-oz. tubes refrigerated
   crescent rolls

16-oz. jar pasteurized process
   cheese sauce
4-oz. can diced green chiles

Combine ground beef and taco seasoning; set aside. Press one tube crescent rolls to cover the bottom of a lightly greased 13"x9" baking pan. Layer beef mixture and pasteurized process cheese sauce on top; sprinkle with green chiles. Arrange remaining package of crescent rolls on top; bake at 400 degrees for 25 to 30 minutes. Makes 8 servings.

Create customized canisters with just a little craft glass paint. Add a flourish of script with the help of stencils or add a simple initial in a color that matches the kitchen. Try etching cream on glass canisters for a touch of frost!

Italian Baked Chicken

Susan Elstrom
Charlotte, NC

Serve with crispy garlic bread and a Caesar salad.

2 lbs. chicken
2 T. butter, melted
1 c. tomato sauce

1 t. dried oregano
1/8 t. garlic powder

Arrange chicken, skin-side down, in an ungreased shallow baking pan; pour butter on top. Bake at 400 degrees for 20 minutes; turn chicken over and bake 20 minutes longer. Pour tomato sauce on top; sprinkle with oregano and garlic powder. Bake until tender and juices run clear when chicken is pierced with a fork, about 20 minutes. Serves 4.

Welcome feathered friends to the garden with a flowerpot birdbath! Stack terra cotta pots in graduated sizes to create the base and use a terra cotta saucer for the bath. Secure everything with hot glue and let dry before setting outside. Paint, rubber stamp or stencil before gluing to add a personal touch.

Buttery Garlic Chicken

Susan VanOrsdel
Abilene, TX

So easy to pop in the oven for dinner...by the time homework's finished, dinner's ready!

2 eggs, beaten
1 c. round buttery crackers,
   crushed
1/2 t. garlic salt

4 boneless, skinless chicken
   breasts
1/2 c. butter, sliced

Place eggs in a shallow bowl; set aside. Mix cracker crumbs and garlic salt in a separate bowl; set aside. Dip chicken in eggs and then coat in crumb mixture. Arrange in an ungreased 13"x9" baking pan; dot with butter. Bake at 375 degrees for 40 minutes or until juices run clear when chicken is pierced with a fork. Makes 4 servings.

Easy Chicken Dinner

Katrina Pierce
Indianapolis, IN

Serve with piping hot biscuits for a complete meal in minutes.

2 10-3/4 oz. cans cream of
   chicken soup
2 10-oz. cans chicken, drained
15-1/4 oz. can peas, drained

8-oz. can sliced mushrooms,
   drained
8-oz. pkg. angel hair pasta,
   cooked

Mix soup, chicken, peas and mushrooms together in a saucepan; heat through. Spoon over hot pasta to serve. Serves 6 to 8.

Host a bridal shower in the garden this spring...use seed packets or tiny starter plants in their own pots as favors!

Skinny Salsa Joes

Marcia Frahm
Urbandale, IA

The longer they simmer, the better they are.
Serve on toasty sandwich buns.

1 lb. ground beef, browned   8-oz. can tomato sauce
1/2 c. salsa   1 T. brown sugar, packed

Combine ingredients in a saucepan; bring to a boil. Reduce heat;
simmer 10 to 15 minutes. Serves 4.

Shredded Chicken

Barbara Wise
Jamestown, OH

This recipe comes from an aunt of ours...she's a fabulous cook and
has had the recipe for a long time. Whether spooned onto
buns or over biscuits, it's delicious.

2 3-lb. cans chicken, drained   1 stalk celery, chopped
1 loaf day-old bread, torn   16-oz. can chicken broth
1/2 c. onion, chopped

Mix first 4 ingredients together; add enough chicken broth until
the consistency of very thick soup is achieved. Spread into an
ungreased 13"x9" baking pan; bake at 350 degrees for 1-1/2 hours.
Serves 24.

Welcome Spring with lacy cotton curtains in the kitchen or
bedroom...tie back with brightly colored fabric strips. Tuck
a bunch of fresh flowers into the tie-backs to
bring a little outside color inside.

mains

Quick & Easy Lasagna

*Tina Stuart
Scottsdale, AZ*

Extra cheesy, this lasagna's a winner!

1 lb. ground beef, browned
3 16-oz. cans tomato sauce
16-oz. pkg. lasagna noodles,
    cooked and divided

2 c. cottage cheese, divided
16-oz. pkg. shredded mozzarella
    cheese, divided

Mix ground beef and tomato sauce together; set aside. Spread 1/4 cup tomato sauce mixture on the bottom of an ungreased 13"x9" baking pan; layer with about half the noodles. Pour half the sauce on top; drop half the cottage cheese by spoonfuls into the sauce. Sprinkle with half the mozzarella cheese; repeat layers beginning with noodles. Bake at 350 degrees until cheese melts, about 20 to 25 minutes. Makes 12 servings.

Fill the tiniest terra cotta pots with votive candles. Lined up on a windowsill, they'll add a warm glow to any kitchen!

45

spring

Creamy Tuna Sandwiches

Phyllis Peters
Three Rivers, MI

A quick, simple lunch to prepare when time is short.

6-oz. can tuna, drained
10-3/4 oz. can cream of
    mushroom soup
1/4 c. milk

1 c. frozen peas, cooked
6 English muffins, halved and
    toasted

Combine ingredients except muffins in a saucepan; bring to a boil. Spoon over bottom halves of English muffins; add top half. Serve warm. Makes 6 servings.

A new twist on placecards! Pick a mini spring bouquet and place in a jelly jar...attach a leaf-shaped tag with the guest's name on it. Just right for garden parties and showers.

46

Wild Chicken & Rice

Kimberly Lyons
Commerce, TX

Mmmm…great with fresh-baked bread and a green salad.

2 6.2-oz. pkgs. instant wild rice
4 boneless, skinless chicken
   breasts, chopped

10-3/4 oz. can cream of
   mushroom soup
8-oz. pkg. frozen mixed
   vegetables, thawed

Gently stir all the ingredients together; add in 3 cups water. Spread into an ungreased 13"x9" baking pan. Bake at 350 degrees until juices run clear when chicken is pierced with a fork, about 45 minutes, stirring occasionally. Serves 4.

Zucchini Patties

Amber Brandt
Tucson, AZ

Serve with a dollop of sour cream and plenty of salt & pepper.

2 onions, chopped
1 zucchini, grated
6 eggs, beaten

2 c. bread crumbs
3 T. fresh parsley, chopped
oil for deep frying

Sauté onions in a skillet until tender; add zucchini and heat for 5 minutes, stirring frequently. Remove from heat and set aside. Pour eggs into a large mixing bowl; mix in onion mixture. Stir in bread crumbs and parsley; set aside. Pour 1/4-inch depth oil into a 12" skillet; heat until hot. Drop spoonfuls of zucchini mixture into hot oil until golden on both sides; drain. Makes 6 to 8 servings.

Spring is when you feel like whistling
even with a shoe full of slush.
- Doug Larson

Chocolate-Marshmallow Pie

Brenda Neal
Taneyville, MO

I received this recipe from a dear friend who's 90 years old...we make this decadent dessert often and enjoy it every time.

16 marshmallows
4 1.45-oz. milk chocolate candy
    bars with almonds

1/2 c. milk
8-oz. carton whipping cream
9-inch graham cracker pie crust

Heat marshmallows, candy bars and milk in a double boiler until marshmallows and chocolate melt; stir often. Remove from heat. Beat whipping cream in a bowl until soft peaks form. Fold whipping cream into marshmallow mixture; spoon into crust. Refrigerate until firm. Serves 8.

Hold an old-fashioned Easter egg hunt right in the backyard! Hide plastic eggs with small gifts or candy along with decorated hard-boiled eggs too. Send the kids out to look for them...what fun!

desserts

Chocolate-Cherry Crunch

Kathy Glass
Neosho, MO

Sprinkle with coconut for a tropical treat!

2 14-1/2 oz. cans cherry pie
    filling
19.8-oz. pkg. fudge brownie
    mix

1/2 c. chopped pecans
1 c. quick-cooking oats,
    uncooked
3/4 c. margarine, melted

Pour pie filling in the bottom of an ungreased 13"x9" baking pan; set
aside. Blend remaining ingredients together until coarse crumbs form;
sprinkle over pie filling. Bake at 350 degrees for 30 minutes. Makes
12 servings.

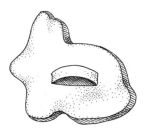

Praline Graham Crackers

Jennifer Eveland-Kupp
Reading, PA

*These cookies make a wonderful gift and they're ready in
less than 30 minutes!*

1 sleeve graham crackers
1 c. butter

1-1/2 c. brown sugar, packed
2 c. pecans

Arrange a single layer of graham crackers in an ungreased
15"x10" jelly-roll pan; set aside. Bring butter, sugar and pecans to
a boil in a heavy saucepan, stirring constantly. Pour over graham
crackers; bake at 350 degrees for 10 minutes. Break into pieces to
serve. Makes about 30 servings.

spring

Cherry Dream Pie

Clara Buckman
Waverly, KY

Perfect for picnics and potlucks.

8-oz. pkg. cream cheese, softened
1/2 c. powdered sugar

8-oz. container frozen whipped topping, thawed
9-inch graham cracker pie crust
14-1/2 oz. can cherry pie filling

Blend cream cheese and powdered sugar together until smooth and creamy; fold in whipped topping. Spread into pie crust forming a well in the center; fill with pie filling. Chill until firm before serving. Makes 8 servings.

Snip new branches from a pussy willow and pair up with the very first forsythia blooms for a cheery spring bouquet...instead of a vase, gather them in a nostalgic pitcher!

desserts

Open-Face Peach Pie

Christy Hughes
Provo, UT

*This favorite pie recipe was handed down to me
from my grandmother.*

1 c. sugar
2 T. cornstarch
9-inch pie crust

6 peaches, pitted, peeled and
halved
1 c. whipping cream

Mix sugar and cornstarch together; spread 3/4 of mixture into pie
crust. Arrange peaches on top; sprinkle with remaining sugar mixture.
Pour cream evenly over peaches; bake at 400 degrees for 10 minutes.
Reduce heat to 350 degrees; bake an additional 40 minutes. Makes
8 servings.

Pineapple Soufflé

Jinny Ruleau
Menominee, MI

Serve slices topped with a dollop of whipped topping!

1/2 c. butter, softened
1 c. sugar

4 slices bread, cubed
20-oz. can crushed pineapple

Combine ingredients together; pour into an ungreased 9"x5" loaf pan.
Bake at 350 degrees for one hour. Makes 8 servings.

Ariel's Lemon Cake

Naomi Cooper
Delaware, OH

So easy to make and just right for enjoying
after a day in the garden.

18-1/4 oz. pkg. lemon cake mix
3/4 c. oil
4 eggs

3-oz. pkg. lemon gelatin mix
3/4 c. water

Add dry cake mix, oil, eggs and gelatin to a large mixing bowl; blend in water until batter is smooth, about 4 minutes. Pour into a lightly greased and floured Bundt® pan; bake at 350 degrees for 40 to 45 minutes. Remove from oven; invert and remove cake. Prick top with a fork; pour glaze over the top while still warm. Makes 10 servings.

Glaze:

2 c. powdered sugar

lemon juice

Blend powdered sugar and enough lemon juice together until mixture reaches a pourable consistency.

Fill a sparkling pitcher with bright lemons and limes...set the pitcher in the center of the kitchen table for a burst of sunshine.

desserts

Pineapple-Cherry Cake

David Flory
Columbus, OH

Serve with whipped topping or ice cream.

20-oz. can crushed pineapple
18-1/4 oz. pkg. yellow cake mix, divided
15-1/2 oz. can pitted cherries, drained

1 c. chopped walnuts or pecans
1 c. butter, melted

Pour pineapple into an ungreased 13"x9" baking pan; spread evenly. Sprinkle half the cake mix on top; spread cherries over cake mix. Sprinkle on remaining cake mix; add nuts. Drizzle with butter; bake at 350 degrees for 45 to 50 minutes. Serves 15.

Grandmother's Pound Cake

Teri Naquin
Melville, LA

An old-fashioned favorite...try it with strawberries on top.

1 c. margarine
1-2/3 c. sugar
5 eggs

1/2 t. vanilla extract
2 c. all-purpose flour

Cream margarine; blend in sugar, eggs and vanilla. Gradually mix in flour; pour into a greased and floured 9"x5" loaf pan. Bake at 300 degrees for one to 1-1/2 hours. Makes 8 to 10 servings.

Dress up pillowcases with whimsical buttons. Just sew them onto the finished edge of the pillow...line up in a row or make a polka-dot pattern with old-fashioned favorites.

Lemon-Lime Cake

Mary Thorn
Bloomfield, MO

For chocolate lovers, substitute a chocolate cake mix, chocolate pudding mix and a can of cola.

18-1/4 oz. pkg. lemon cake mix
4 eggs
3-1/2 oz. pkg. instant lemon
    pudding mix

3/4 c. oil
10-oz. can lemon-lime soda

Combine all ingredients; mix well. Pour into a lightly greased 13"x9" baking pan. Bake at 350 degrees for 40 minutes. Cool; frost as desired. Refrigerate until ready to serve. Makes 15 to 18 servings.

Buttercups and daisies,
Oh, the pretty flowers;
Coming 'ere the Springtime,
To tell of sunny hours.
- Mary Howitt

Coconut Clouds

Charlene Smith
Lombard, IL

*For extra sparkle, top with a candied cherry and sprinkle
with sugar before baking.*

3/4 c. sugar
2-1/2 c. flaked coconut
2 egg whites, beaten

1 t. vanilla extract
1/8 t. salt

Combine ingredients together; blend until soft peaks form. Drop by
tablespoonfuls, one inch apart, on a greased baking sheet; bake at
350 degrees for 15 to 20 minutes. Cool on a wire rack. Store in an
airtight container. Makes 15 to 20.

Butterball Cookies

Dorothy Adams
Chesaning, MI

Use real butter in this recipe for melt-in-your-mouth taste.

2 c. butter, softened
1 c. plus 2 T. brown sugar,
  packed

1 t. vanilla extract
4-1/2 c. all-purpose flour
sugar

Blend butter until fluffy; add brown sugar and vanilla, mixing well.
Blend in flour; set aside, uncovered, for 24 hours at room temperature.
Roll dough into one-inch balls; roll in sugar. Bake on ungreased
baking sheets at 350 degrees for 15 to 20 minutes. Makes 8 dozen.

For a quick treat bag for school or church, snip off the top
2/3 of a paper grocery sack with pinking shears. Place treats
inside and fasten it closed with some fun stickers...try
using a hole punch and then weaving a ribbon through!

Peanut Butter-Chocolate Bars

Eileen Blass
Catawissa, PA

Top with marshmallow creme for s'more fun!

1 c. creamy peanut butter
1 c. butter, melted
1 c. graham cracker crumbs

16-oz. pkg. powdered sugar
2 c. semi-sweet chocolate chips,
   melted

Combine first 4 ingredients together in a large mixing bowl; mix well using a wooden spoon. Press into the bottom of a well-greased 15"x10" jelly-roll pan; pour melted chocolate evenly over crust. Refrigerate for 15 minutes; score into bars but leave in pan. Refrigerate until firm; slice completely through scores and serve cold. Makes 25 to 30.

Cookie cutter topiaries make sweet centerpieces for spring flings. Just secure a dowel in a terra cotta pot using sand or floral foam, glue a flower-shaped cookie cutter on top and tie on a ribbon for the "leaves."

desserts

Speedy Peanut Butter Cookies

Tiffany Leiter
Midland, MI

That's correct...there's no flour in these cookies!

1 c. sugar   1 egg
1 c. creamy peanut butter

Blend ingredients together; set aside for 5 minutes. Scoop dough with a small ice cream scoop; place 2 inches apart on ungreased baking sheets. Make a crisscross pattern on top of each cookie using the tines of a fork; bake at 350 degrees for 10 to 12 minutes. Cool on baking sheets for 5 minutes; remove to wire rack to finish cooling. Makes 12 to 15.

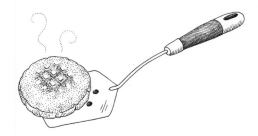

BIG Chocolate Cookies

Lynda Thomassen
Austin, TX

Place a crème de menthe thin on top of each cookie as soon as they come out of the oven...let melt and swirl with a knife for a green and chocolate marble effect.

2 18-1/4 oz. pkgs. chocolate   3 eggs
   cake mix   3/4 c. oil
19.8-oz. pkg. brownie mix

Mix ingredients together along with 3/4 cup water in a large mixing bowl; drop 3 inches apart by tablespoonfuls onto ungreased baking sheets. Bake at 325 degrees for 8 to 10 minutes. Makes about 6 dozen.

spring

Gooey Brownies

Shirley Robbins
Barnegat, NJ

Enjoy them glazed or plain...especially good when served with a tall glass of cold milk.

19.8-oz. pkg. brownie mix
12-oz. pkg. chocolate and
  peanut butter chips

1 c. sour cream
1 c. chopped pecans

Prepare brownie mix following package directions; add remaining ingredients, stirring well. Spread into a greased 13"x9" baking pan; bake at 350 degrees for 35 minutes. Cool; frost with glaze, if desired. Makes 24.

Chocolate Glaze:

6-oz. pkg. semi-sweet chocolate   3 T. butter
  chips

Melt chips and butter together in a double boiler; stir until smooth.

Fill an old-fashioned blue canning jar with freshly roasted coffee beans...attach a hand-stamped or printed label. Tuck into a basket with some flavored non-dairy creamer, a few mugs and some yummy brownies. A gift coffee lovers will enjoy!

Summer

Oh, the summer night
has a smile of light...
- B.W. Proctor

Summer

Chicken-Salsa Dip

Margaret Collins
Clarendon Hills, IL

This recipe has been floating around our Bunco group for awhile...I'm not sure who originated it but we all love it!

8-oz. jar salsa, divided
8-oz. pkg. cream cheese,
   softened

8-oz. pkg. shredded
   Mexican-blend cheese
2 to 3 boneless, skinless chicken
   breasts, cooked and diced

Blend half the salsa with the cream cheese; spread on the bottom of an ungreased 9" pie pan. Top with remaining salsa; sprinkle with cheese and chicken. Bake at 350 degrees for 25 minutes. Serves 8.

Taco Dip

Maria Stiffler
South Bend, IN

Enjoy this dip with tortilla or corn chips.

16-oz. pkg. pasteurized process
   cheese spread
2 8-oz. pkgs. cream cheese,
   softened

16-oz. jar salsa
1-1/4 oz. pkg. taco seasoning
   mix
1 lb. ground beef, browned

Melt cheeses in a slow cooker; set aside. While melting, combine salsa, taco seasoning and beef; stir into cheese mixture. Heat on low setting for 20 minutes. Serves 8.

Search flea markets for painted windowpanes (with glass removed) for a ready-made frame...use it to display colorful shells or starfish gathered on summer vacation!

Tamale Pie

Kelly Cook
Dunedin, FL

Ready-made tamales make this pie oh-so quick.

15-oz. can chili, divided
10-oz. pkg. corn chips, divided
1 onion, minced and divided

2 13-1/2 oz. cans beef tamales,
    chopped and divided
2 c. shredded Cheddar cheese,
    divided

Spread one cup chili in the bottom of a greased 2-quart casserole dish;
layer half the corn chips, half the onion and one can tamales on top.
Sprinkle with half the cheese; repeat layers. Cover and bake at
350 degrees for one hour. Let cool for 10 minutes before serving.
Makes 12 servings.

*H*osting a summer get-together? Put together topiary place
markers...mount tiny birdhouses on dowels and then secure in
pretty painted pots. Send them home as favors too!

summer

Sesame Spread

Jennifer Kirby
Delaware, OH

*This dip is my favorite...I wouldn't even look at cottage cheese
until my roommate introduced me to this recipe!*

8-oz. pkg. cream cheese,
   softened
2 c. cottage cheese

1 T. sesame seed, toasted
1 t. dried parsley
1 t. garlic salt

Mix cream cheese and cottage cheese together; add sesame seed,
parsley and garlic salt. Mix until well blended. Makes about 3 cups.

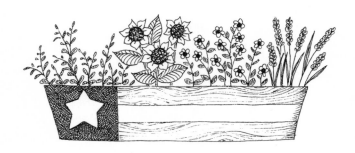

*Herb gardens smell wonderful on a kitchen windowsill...why not
give one to a special friend? Place individually potted herbs inside
a wooden crate or a retro-style tin. How thoughtful!*

appetizers

Granny's Zesty Dip

Malinda Ahmann
Dubuque, IA

Guests will never guess the secret ingredient!

2 8-oz. pkgs. cream cheese,
  softened
4-oz. can diced green chiles

2/3 c. peach jam
8-oz. pkg. shredded Cheddar
  cheese

Blend cream cheese, chiles and jam together until smooth; spread into
a shallow serving dish. Sprinkle with cheese; cover and refrigerate until
chilled. Makes about 3-1/2 cups.

Spunky Spinach Dip

Beverly Weppler
Atlantic, IA

Whether served with tortilla chips, fresh veggies or
bread cubes, it's irresistible.

2 c. salsa
2 c. shredded Monterey Jack
  cheese
8-oz. pkg. cream cheese,
  softened and cubed

10-oz. pkg. frozen chopped
  spinach, thawed and drained
1 c. pitted olives, chopped

Mix all ingredients together; stir well. Place in a microwave-safe bowl;
microwave on medium setting until heated through. Serves about 10.

For graduation, roll up napkins like diplomas and tie with ribbons.
Scatter framed photos of the graduate at
various ages on the table.

Tangy Cheese Ball

Ramey Norton
Lancaster, KY

Chopped ham works well in this recipe too.

1/2 sweet onion, minced
2 8-oz. pkgs. cream cheese,
  softened

1 t. Worcestershire sauce
2 2-1/2 oz. pkgs. dried, chipped
  beef, chopped

Combine ingredients; mix well. Form into a ball and wrap in plastic wrap. Refrigerate until chilled. Serves 8.

Pop a candle in an old blue canning jar, fill the bottom with sand and light. Lined up around a deck or down a walkway, they'll look so pretty on a summer night.

appetizers

Cream Cheese-Crab Dip

Sharon Gardner
Iberia, MO

Sprinkle with Parmesan cheese just before serving, if you like.

2 8-oz. pkgs. cream cheese,
   softened
1 c. sour cream
1/2 t. onion powder

2 green onions, chopped
6-oz. pkg. imitation crabmeat,
   chopped

Combine cream cheese, sour cream and onion powder; fold in onions and crab. Mix well; chill. Makes about 3-1/2 cups.

Avocado Dip

Susie Rogers
Puyallup, WA

Yummy with toasted pita triangles or bagel chips.

2 avocados, pitted, peeled and
   chopped
8-oz. pkg. cream cheese,
   softened

1/4 c. mayonnaise
1/2 to 1 t. garlic salt

Blend all ingredients together; cover and chill until serving. Makes about 2 cups.

Breezy days call for flirty curtains in the kitchen! Whip up a fun addition with cotton napkins...2 or 3 per panel, depending on the size of the window. Just tack a rod pocket in the top of one and sew others onto the first with dainty buttons.

Artichoke Seafood Dip

*Sharon Schamber
Lakewood, WA*

Serve with hearty wheat crackers.

1 c. mayonnaise
1 c. grated Parmesan cheese
14-oz. can artichoke hearts,
    drained and diced

1/2 c. flaked crabmeat
1 round loaf sourdough bread

Combine first 4 ingredients together in a microwave-safe bowl;
microwave on high until mixture bubbles. Hollow out round loaf of
bread, cubing and reserving removed bread for dipping; pour dip into
hollowed-out loaf to serve. Serve warm. Serves 8.

Turn a vacation memento into a candle that can be enjoyed year
'round...place a wick in the center of a scallop shell and
fill with melted wax. So easy!

appetizers

Cream Cheese Toasties

Jayne Lammers
Quincy, IL

May be made ahead of time and frozen...great as an appetizer or just broil a few for a snack!

1 loaf sliced bread, crusts
   trimmed
2 8-oz. pkgs. cream cheese,
   softened
6 T. mayonnaise

6 scallions, finely chopped
10 drops hot pepper sauce
Optional: grated Parmesan
   cheese

Toast one side of bread slices under the broiler; cut each slice into quarters. Combine remaining ingredients; spread on untoasted sides. Sprinkle with Parmesan cheese, if desired; broil until golden. Serves 8.

Decorate the garden with weatherproof collectibles...flea market finds can include vintage-style watering cans, old-fashioned spinning sprinklers or even a weathered wooden bench.

Summer

Suzanne Price
Nebo, NC

Fruity Cheese Ball

*Serve with graham crackers or spread on thin slices
of pound cake...yum!*

2 8-oz. pkgs. cream cheese,
  softened
3-1/2 oz. pkg. instant vanilla
  pudding mix

15-oz. can fruit cocktail, drained
Garnish: chopped pecans

Mix cream cheese, pudding and fruit cocktail together. Form into a ball;
roll in pecans. Wrap in plastic wrap; refrigerate overnight. Serves 8.

Comb flea markets for plastic or metal cafeteria trays in soft pastel
colors. Their no-frills retro look will not only be right at home
at barbecues and other backyard gatherings, they'll
look pretty on a dresser or a buffet.

soups & breads

Sparkling Berry Soup

Jo Ann

"Berry" refreshing...use your favorite in this recipe.

6 c. berries, stems removed
1 c. orange juice
3 T. lemon juice
1/2 c. sugar

2 c. sparkling water
Optional: ice cream or frozen
   yogurt

Purée berries and juices together; pour into a punch bowl. Stir in sugar and sparkling water; cover and refrigerate for 2 hours. Ladle into chilled serving bowls; top with a scoop of ice cream or frozen yogurt, if desired. Makes 6 to 8 servings.

Strawberry Soup

Cheryl Hatfield
Knoxville, TN

Serve with whipped topping instead of yogurt for a fun twist.

4 c. strawberries, hulled and
   diced
1/2 c. sugar

1-1/2 c. orange juice
1 c. vanilla yogurt

Purée strawberries, sugar and orange juice; strain through a cheesecloth, discarding solids. Pour into serving bowls; spoon a dollop of yogurt on top. Makes 2 to 4 servings.

Red, white and true blue! Use mini flags as plant pokes or along a backyard walkway...hang patriotic bunting from a porch or fence to show patriotic pride year 'round.

Baked Potato-Cheddar Soup

Leah Hickman
Pataskala, OH

We like it sprinkled with bacon bits and sliced green onions too!

2 10-3/4 oz. cans cream of
   potato soup
2 15-oz. cans sliced potatoes,
   drained

1 pt. whipping cream
1 c. milk
1 c. shredded Cheddar cheese

Pour soups, potatoes, whipping cream and milk into an ungreased
2-quart casserole dish; mix well. Cover and bake at 400 degrees for
45 minutes to one hour. Ladle into serving bowls; sprinkle with
cheese. Makes 6 servings.

Search out nostalgic yellowware soup tureens and matching bowls
at antique shops and auctions. They'll add an old-fashioned
flair to the dinner table or buffet.

Corn Fritters

Marty Darling
Coshocton, OH

Tasty with a meal or just as a snack!

8-1/2 oz. can creamed corn	1/2 t. baking powder
8-3/4 oz. can corn	7 T. all-purpose flour
2 eggs, beaten	oil for deep frying

Combine first 5 ingredients; mix well. Drop by tablespoonfuls into hot oil; heat until golden. Turn and heat other side until golden also. Makes 4 to 6 servings.

Overrun with tomatoes, corn and peppers from the garden?
Pick out the best of the bunch, tuck into a basket or
vintage pail and surprise a neighbor!

Easy Broccoli-Cheese Soup

Jennifer Pohto
Willoughby, OH

Add cooked, cubed ham or diced potatoes and watch it disappear!

1/4 c. onion, chopped
10-oz. pkg. frozen broccoli cuts,
  cooked
8-oz. pkg. cream cheese, cubed

12-oz. pkg. pasteurized process
  cheese spread, cubed
2 c. milk

Sauté onion until tender; add to a saucepan. Add remaining ingredients; heat until cheeses melt, stirring constantly. Makes 5 to 6 servings.

Homestyle Biscuit Bread

Alysea Frampton
Richlands, NC

An old-fashioned favorite.

1 c. milk
2 c. self-rising flour

1/2 c. oil

Combine ingredients; mix well. Pour into a hot, well-greased 10" cast iron skillet. Bake at 400 degrees for 18 to 20 minutes; slice into wedges to serve. Makes 8 servings.

soups & breads

Nothing-To-It Chili

Peggy Merman
Louisville, KY

Serve over spaghetti for Cincinnati-style chili.

1 lb. ground beef
1 onion, chopped
1-1/4 oz. pkg. chili seasoning
   mix

15-oz. can tomatoes
29-oz. can hot chili beans

Sauté ground beef and onion together in a 12" skillet until beef is browned and onion is tender; drain. Add remaining ingredients; stir well. Simmer over low heat for 25 minutes. Makes 2 quarts.

Simple Baked Bean Soup

Barbara Ture
Montvale, NJ

So easy and guaranteed to warm their tummies.

28-oz. can baked beans
28-oz. can stewed tomatoes

pepper to taste

Combine ingredients in a saucepan; heat until boiling. Reduce heat; simmer for 15 minutes. Makes 4 servings.

Float cut blooms in water for a 5-minute centerpiece! Roses, sunflowers and dahlias are so pretty in a cut glass bowl or teacup.

Summer

Seasoned Oyster Crackers

Jen Sell
Farmington, MN

*So good to snack on by themselves or sprinkled
into homemade soups and stews.*

1-1/2 c. oil
2 1-oz. pkgs. ranch seasoning
   and salad dressing mix
1 T. lemon pepper
1 T. dill weed
2 10-oz. pkgs. oyster crackers

Whisk first 4 ingredients together; pour over oyster crackers. Toss gently; spread on an ungreased baking sheet. Bake at 225 degrees for one hour, stirring every 15 minutes. Makes 24 servings.

Put everyone's favorite summertime photos together in a scrapbook to be enjoyed year 'round! Add postcards from family trips, ticket stubs from the county fair and other mementos too.

soups & breads

Cheesy Crab Soup

Kate Conroy
Bethlehem, PA

A rich and filling soup...enjoy with crusty bread and a tossed salad.

2 10-3/4 oz. cans Cheddar cheese soup	1 lb. crabmeat, cooked
2 12-oz. cans evaporated milk	1/2 c. butter, melted
	1 t. seafood seasoning

Heat soup and milk in a heavy saucepan; stir until creamy and smooth. Add crabmeat and butter; stir constantly. Mix in seasoning; heat through but do not boil. Serve immediately. Serves 4 to 6.

Snuggle in under the stars no matter what the weather! Look for architectural stars at auctions or pick up reproductions at the craft store...paint them or leave them rustic for a primitive touch. Use epoxy to attach picture hangers to the back and then group them over an old-fashioned iron headboard.

Summer

A to Z Veggie Delight

Brenda Doak
Delaware, OH

A favorite when served over rice or with pork chops.

2 c. asparagus, chopped
2 c. zucchini, peeled and cubed
2 T. butter

1 c. sliced mushrooms
1/8 t. dill weed

Sauté asparagus and zucchini in butter until crisp-tender; add mushrooms and dill weed, stirring until mushrooms are golden and warmed through. Makes 6 servings.

Look for old wooden boxes with partitions...they were often used to hold beverage bottles separately. They make great containers for herb gardens or for a sampling of annuals.

Crispy Spinach Cakes

Beth Burnett
Salem, IN

This is one of the few things my father made from scratch when we were young. He remembers my grandmother making them for him when he was growing up in the 1930's and 1940's.

14-1/2 oz. can spinach, drained
3/4 c. bread crumbs
1 egg

1/2 to 3/4 c. milk
oil for deep frying

Mix all ingredients except oil together; set aside. Heat 1/2-inch depth oil in a heavy skillet; drop dough by tablespoonfuls into skillet. Heat for 4 to 6 minutes until golden; flip and heat other side. Makes 10 to 15.

Green Bean Bake

Jennie Parker
Rochester, NY

Smells so good while baking...reminds me of many family gatherings.

5 14-1/2 oz. cans green beans,
    drained
5 slices bacon, diced

1 onion, chopped
1 c. catsup
1 c. brown sugar, packed

Combine ingredients; spread in an ungreased 13"x9" baking pan. Bake at 250 degrees for 3 hours. Serves 8 to 10.

Summer

Pepper-Onion Steak Sauté

Barb Jones
Fort Dodge, IA

Spoon on top of grilled ribeye steaks right before serving.

1 onion, sliced
1 green pepper, sliced
8-oz. pkg. sliced mushrooms

2 T. butter
minced garlic to taste

Sauté ingredients together until tender. Makes 4 servings.

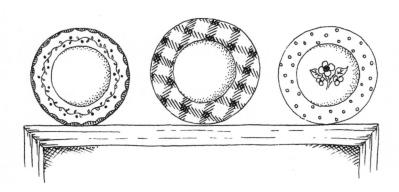

Pick up mismatched dessert plates in similar sizes at antique shops
and auctions or find a few in Grandma's attic! Hang them
over the kitchen doorway for a cottage touch.

Linguini & Veggie Salad

Jenny Dreisbach
York, PA

Cool and crispy...just right for picnics!

16-oz. pkg. linguini, cooked
8-oz. bottle Italian salad
   dressing

1 tomato, diced
1 cucumber, diced
3 T. salad seasoning

Rinse linguini in cold water; drain and place in a serving dish. Pour Italian salad dressing on top; mix well. Fold in tomato, cucumber and salad seasoning. Mix well; cover and refrigerate for 24 hours. Makes 8 to 10 servings.

Pork & Bean Salad

Suzi Bryant
Juliette, GA

So tasty alongside hamburgers, steaks or grilled chicken.

2 16-oz. cans pork & beans
1 onion, minced
1 tomato, chopped

2 to 3 T. mayonnaise
celery salt to taste

Combine ingredients together; cover and chill before serving. Makes 4 servings.

Pepper & Corn Salad

*Lynn Newton
Oklahoma City, OK*

*Toss in some cherry tomatoes, sliced cucumbers or
any of your favorite veggies!*

2 15-1/4 oz. cans corn, drained
1 bunch green onions, chopped
1 green pepper, chopped

5-oz. jar stuffed olives, drained
and sliced
8-oz. bottle Italian salad
dressing

Fold ingredients together; cover and chill overnight. Makes
6 servings.

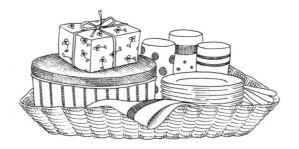

Frozen Cucumber Salad

*Millie Kodor
Fostoria, OH*

*A quick & easy way to use up all those extra cucumbers
from the summer harvest.*

2 qts. cucumbers, peeled
and sliced
2 onions, sliced

1 T. salt
1 c. vinegar
1-1/4 c. sugar

Combine cucumbers, onions and salt; set aside for 4 hours. Add
vinegar and sugar to a heavy saucepan; heat over medium heat until
sugar dissolves. Drain cucumbers; add to vinegar mixture. Spoon into
a freezer-safe container with a lid; freeze. Remove from freezer to
partially thaw before serving. Makes 8 to 10 servings.

Creamy Broccoli & Cheese

Stella Hickman
Galloway, OH

A dear friend shared her mom's recipe with me…it comes from an Amish area in northeastern Ohio.

4 10-oz. pkgs. frozen broccoli
1 c. butter, divided
3-1/2 c. corn flake cereal,
   crushed

12-oz. pkg. cream cheese, cubed
   and divided
12 slices American cheese

Prepare broccoli according to package directions; drain well and set aside. Melt 1/2 cup butter; toss with cereal and set aside. Stir cream cheese and remaining butter together in a small saucepan over low heat until melted; remove from heat and set aside. Layer half the broccoli in an ungreased 2-quart casserole dish; spread half the cream cheese mixture on top. Arrange 6 slices of cheese on top; sprinkle with half the cereal mixture. Repeat layers one time; bake, uncovered, at 350 degrees for one hour. Makes 12 to 15 servings.

Add a fresh coat of paint to small mismatched frames and then glue a few favorite floral patterns to the cardboard insert of the frame. Voilà...flowers that won't fade! Hang together over a mantel or in the hallway.

Summer

Mom Gowdy's Ambrosia

Linda Day
Wall, NJ

Always looks so pretty when served in clear glass dessert cups.

2 11-oz. cans mandarin
   oranges, drained
2 13-oz. cans pineapple chunks,
   drained

1 c. flaked coconut
2 c. sour cream
2 c. mini marshmallows

Mix all ingredients in a serving bowl; cover and refrigerate. Serves
8 to 10.

Old-Fashioned Fruit Salad Dressing

Susan Skinner
Mapleton, UT

*Our favorite when poured over a bowl of mandarin oranges, pine-
apple chunks, raspberries, tart cherries and mini marshmallows.*

2 eggs
1/4 c. pineapple juice
2 T. sugar

1 T. butter
1 pt. whipping cream

Heat first 4 ingredients together in a heavy saucepan over medium
heat until mixture boils; reduce heat, whisking until mixture thickens.
Set aside to cool to room temperature. Whip whipping cream until soft
peaks form; fold into cooled dressing. Cover and refrigerate until
serving. Makes about 2 cups.

Liven up terra cotta pots with acrylic paints...add brightly colored
polka dots, a whimsical wavy line or stamp the
name of the flower planted inside!

Blueberry Cloud Fruit Salad

Carol Volz Begley
Beaver, PA

Fluffy, fruity and fantastic!

3 3-oz. pkgs. strawberry gelatin
   mix
14-1/2 oz. can blueberries, juice
   reserved

15-1/4 oz. can crushed
   pineapple, juice reserved
3 c. sour cream

Dissolve gelatin in 3 cups boiling water; add reserved fruit juices. Chill until thickened; blend in sour cream. Fold in fruit; chill until firm. Serves 6 to 8.

Grape Salad

Cindy Calvert
Lubbock, TX

Sprinkle with cinnamon and sugar if you'd like.

1 c. brown sugar, packed
1 c. sour cream
1 t. almond extract

1 c. chopped pecans
2 c. seedless grapes, halved

Combine first 3 ingredients together; fold in pecans and grapes, mixing gently until well coated. Cover and refrigerate until serving. Makes 4 to 6 servings.

Add some spark to Fourth of July picnics by topping the table off with whimsical fireworks. Paint some assorted dowels with red, white and blue stripes, stamp on a star or 2 and add a jute "fuse"...what fun!

Summer

Chunky Tomato-Avocado Salad

Alma Evans
Patrick AFB, FL

*Let it sit for at least 2 hours if you don't
have time to refrigerate overnight.*

1 avocado, pitted, peeled and
    cubed
3 plum tomatoes, chopped

1/4 c. sweet onion, chopped
1 T. fresh cilantro, chopped
2 to 3 T. lemon juice

Gently stir ingredients together; cover and refrigerate overnight. Makes
4 servings.

Southwestern 3-Bean Salad

Jane Gates
Saginaw, MI

If you like it spicy, add a few drops of hot pepper sauce.

19-oz. can black bean soup,
    drained
1/2 c. red wine vinegar
15-1/2 oz. can kidney beans,
    drained

16-oz. jar salsa
15-1/2 oz. can navy beans,
    drained

Mix ingredients together; cover and refrigerate until serving. Serves 6.

Fill muffin tins with a
little coarse salt and
nestle bright votives in
the centers for an instant
centerpiece in any season!

Salads & Sides

Island Chicken Salad

Carol Hickman
Kingsport, TN

Pile high on fresh croissants.

10-oz. can chunk white chicken,
    drained
8-oz. can crushed pineapple,
    drained

2 stalks celery, diced
8-oz. pkg. cream cheese,
    softened
2 T. mayonnaise

Mix all ingredients together until well blended; chill. Makes 4 servings.

Summertime Pasta Salad

Lisa Arvin
Newburgh, IN

Served warm or cold, it's a family favorite.

8-oz. pkg. tri-color rotini,
    cooked
1 cucumber, chopped
2 tomatoes, chopped

6 to 8 mini carrots, chopped
8-oz. bottle Italian salad
    dressing

Rinse pasta in cold water; drain and pour into a serving bowl. Add
remaining ingredients; toss to coat. Serves 4.

15-Minute Parmesan Pasta

Judy Spahn
Canton, IL

For a complete meal, add grilled chicken breast and
your favorite cooked veggies.

8-oz. pkg. pasta, cooked
1 clove garlic, minced

1/4 c. olive oil
3/4 c. grated Parmesan cheese

Place pasta in a large serving bowl; keep warm. Sauté garlic in olive oil until golden and tender; pour over pasta. Add cheese; toss gently to coat. Serve immediately. Makes 4 servings.

Summery Tomato-Basil Pie

Lori Carr
Gooseberry Patch

So easy to toss together...just watch it disappear!

8-oz. box buttermilk biscuit
  baking mix
1 tomato, sliced
12 fresh basil leaves

6-oz. pkg. shredded asiago
  cheese
1 c. mayonnaise

Mix baking mix according to manufacturer's directions; press dough into an ungreased 8" pie pan. Layer tomato slices and then basil leaves on top of dough; set aside. Combine cheese and mayonnaise in a mixing bowl; blend well. Spread cheese mixture over top, covering all tomato slices and basil. Bake at 350 degrees for 30 to 40 minutes. Slice into wedges to serve. Serves 4 to 6.

Fresh Tomato Spaghetti Sauce

Vickie

The secret ingredient is mint!

4 cloves garlic, minced
3 T. olive oil, divided
3 lbs. tomatoes, peeled and
   chopped

1 T. fresh mint leaves, chopped
garlic salt and pepper to taste

Place garlic and 2 tablespoons olive oil in a 12" skillet; heat over low heat until garlic is tender, about 2 minutes. Increase heat to high and sauté until golden, about 10 seconds. Add tomatoes, stirring occasionally until the sauce is thick and chunky, about 10 minutes. Remove from heat; stir in mint and season with garlic salt and pepper. Pour over warm spaghetti to serve. Serves 4.

No-Fuss Tomato Sauce

Jeff Doak
Delaware, OH

A tasty sauce to complement any pasta dish...ready in minutes!

28-oz. can crushed tomatoes
2 T. olive oil

2 cloves garlic, minced
salt and pepper to taste

Combine ingredients in a heavy saucepan; simmer until thickened, about 20 minutes. Makes 3-1/2 cups.

Instant charm! Cover everyday frames, mirrors and boxes with squares of bright scrapbook paper, vintage fabric or even wallpaper remnants found at hardware stores. Create a patchwork effect with larger pieces and decoupage a chair, table or headboard.

Fruity Baked Chicken

Jennifer Holmes
Philadelphia, PA

Serve over rice with a side of asparagus spears...yum.

2 T. olive oil
6 boneless, skinless chicken
   breasts
3 lemons, halved

3 oranges, halved
1 apple, cored, peeled and
   chopped

Coat the bottom of a 13"x9" baking pan with olive oil; arrange chicken breasts on top. Squeeze juice from one lemon and one orange over chicken; set aside. Slice remaining lemons and oranges into wedges; cut these in half. Arrange around and on top of chicken breasts; add apple. Cover and bake at 375 degrees for one hour and 45 minutes; uncover for last 1/2 hour of baking. Makes 6 servings.

Hawaiian Chicken

Tamara Fennell
FPO, AE

For an extra-yummy treat, add a thin slice of grilled ham and top with provolone cheese before baking.

3 c. pineapple chunks,
   undrained
1 c. soy sauce

1 t. ground ginger
1/4 t. garlic, chopped
4 lbs. split chicken breasts

Mix all ingredients except chicken together. Add chicken; marinate for 4 hours in the refrigerator. Grill chicken until browned; arrange in an ungreased 13"x9" baking pan. Bake, uncovered, at 325 degrees for one hour. Serves 4.

mains

Barbecue Chicken Kabobs

Robin Hill
Rochester, NY

As soon as our local farmers' market opens, I look for my "chicken lady." She brings the freshest, most flavorful chicken for these kabobs.

4 boneless, skinless chicken
   breasts, cubed
1 green pepper, cut into 2-inch
   squares
1 sweet onion, cut into wedges

1 red pepper, cut into 2-inch
   squares
1 c. favorite barbecue sauce
4 to 6 skewers

Thread chicken, green pepper, onion and red pepper pieces alternately onto skewers. Place kabobs on a lightly oiled grill pan over medium heat. Cook for 12 to 15 minutes, turning and brushing frequently with barbecue sauce, until chicken juices run clear and vegetables are tender. Serves 4 to 6.

Setting out summer annuals? Try planting them in an old red wagon for a touch of childhood charm! Be sure to drill holes in the bottom and add some gravel for even drainage.

Summer

BBQ Slow-Cooker Chicken

Elisha Wiggins
Suwanee, GA

A delicious recipe from my grandma!

4 boneless, skinless chicken
   breasts
3/4 c. chicken broth

1 c. barbecue sauce
1 sweet onion, sliced
salt and pepper to taste

Place all ingredients in a slow cooker; stir gently. Heat on
high setting for 3 hours or on low setting for 6 to 7 hours. Makes
4 servings.

*H*ave star-spangled barbecues all Summer long! Use
red, white and blue tableware along with mini flags
and sparklers in the centerpieces.

mains

Baked Barbecue Chicken

Heather Riley
Johnston, IA

*This was one of the first dishes I made for my husband when we were
newlyweds...he still requests it 7 years later!*

4 boneless, skinless chicken
   breasts
1 c. all-purpose flour
6 to 7 bacon slices

8-oz. can mushroom pieces,
   drained
1-1/2 c. barbecue sauce

Coat chicken breasts in flour; arrange in an ungreased 13"x9" baking
pan. Lay bacon across tops of chicken; bake at 400 degrees for
45 minutes. Drain. Add mushroom pieces; pour barbecue sauce on
top. Bake 15 minutes longer. Serves 4.

BBQ Chicken Quiche

Barbara Anderson
San Antonio, TX

Refrigerated pie crust makes this one quick quiche!

4 eggs
1 c. half-and-half
1 c. barbecued chicken, cubed

1/2 c. onion, finely chopped
9-inch pie crust

Combine first 4 ingredients; mix well. Pour into pie crust; bake at
350 degrees for 40 minutes. Makes 8 servings.

Keep an eye out for vintage-style Shaker bottles once used for
storing dried herbs. They'll look so pretty filled with
dried lentils or beans on a kitchen shelf.

Summer

Summertime Salmon Cakes

Gina Burnett
Tampa, FL

Enjoy with a fresh green salad and tall glass of lemonade!

2 6-oz. cans salmon, drained   salt and pepper
2 eggs   olive oil
10 saltine crackers, crushed

Mix first 4 ingredients together; form into patties. Heat both sides in hot oil in a skillet until golden. Serves 2 to 4.

For a whimsical party favor, roll a doily into a cone and glue in place. Fill with a few flower sprigs and wrapped candy then hang on the back of each chair.

Spicy Salmon Marinade

Lynda McCormick
Burkburnett, TX

Marinate salmon filets for one hour, then grill to perfection...so easy!

1/3 c. soy sauce
1/3 c. frozen orange juice
   concentrate, thawed

1 T. sesame oil
1/4 c. honey
1 t. red pepper flakes

Combine soy sauce, juice, oil, honey and pepper; mix well. Makes about one cup.

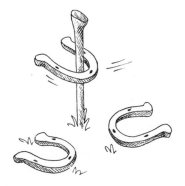

Tuna Steak Marinade

Susan Curtis
Greenlawn, NY

Marinate tuna steaks for at least an hour before grilling.

1/4 c. olive oil
3 scallions, chopped

1 t. dried rosemary
2 cloves garlic, minced

Combine ingredients together; mix well.

For the laughter of children who fumble barefooted and
bareheaded in the Summer...
- Carl Sandberg

Crunchy Corn Chip Chicken

Tegan Reeves
Auburndale, FL

So quick to whip up!

6 boneless, skinless chicken
  breasts
10-3/4 oz. can cream of
  chicken soup
2 c. shredded Cheddar cheese,
  divided

1-1/4 oz. pkg. taco seasoning
  mix
2 c. barbecue corn chips,
  crushed

Arrange chicken in an ungreased 13"x9" baking pan; set aside.
Combine soup, one cup cheese and taco seasoning together; spread
over chicken. Bake at 450 degrees for 45 minutes; sprinkle with corn
chips and remaining cheese. Return to oven; bake until cheese melts,
about 5 minutes. Makes 6 servings.

Sew an easy pouch or buy cloth bags at the craft store to fill with
dried flowers or fragrant herbs. Simple sachets are so pretty
tied with a satin ribbon or raffia!

mains

Lemony Garlic Chicken

Diana Zylicz
Cypress, TX

Serve with wild rice or sautéed vegetables.

3 cloves garlic, minced
1/4 c. butter
6-oz. can frozen lemonade
    concentrate, thawed

3 lbs. chicken
salt and pepper to taste

Sauté garlic in butter until golden and tender; remove from heat. Stir in lemonade; set aside. Season chicken with salt and pepper; coat with lemonade mixture. Grill or broil until juices run clear when chicken is pierced with a fork; baste frequently with lemonade mixture. Makes 4 servings.

Savory Cranberry Chicken

Wayne Smith
Wesson, MS

Perfect for dinner parties...what a pretty presentation!

6 boneless, skinless chicken
    breasts
16-oz. can whole berry
    cranberry sauce

8-oz. bottle French salad
    dressing
1-1/2 oz. pkg. onion soup mix

Arrange chicken in an ungreased 13"x9" baking pan; set aside. Combine remaining ingredients together; mix well. Pour over chicken breasts; cover with aluminum foil. Bake at 350 degrees for one hour. Makes 6 servings.

Set a glass tabletop on a birdbath for a whimsical side table...fill the inside with vintage seed packets, flowery garden gloves and a found birds' nest. Perfect for a patio or porch!

Summer

EZ-Fix Burgers

Mickey Johnson
Naperville, IL

Dinner in a pocket...fun for the little ones!

1 lb. ground beef
salt and pepper to taste

16-oz. pkg. frozen mixed
vegetables, thawed

Form ground beef into patties; season with salt and pepper. Brown until nearly done. Place one patty in the center of a square of aluminum foil large enough to form a tent around the patty; spoon desired amount of vegetables on top. Fold edges of aluminum foil together to form an enclosed pocket; repeat with remaining patties. Place on a baking sheet; bake at 350 degrees for 20 to 25 minutes. Open carefully to allow steam to escape. Makes about 4 servings.

Cheeseburger Bake

Jennifer Dutcher
Lewis Center, OH

A hearty meal in itself!

8-oz. tube refrigerated crescent
rolls
1 lb. ground beef, browned

1-1/4 oz. pkg. taco seasoning
mix
15-oz. can tomato sauce
2 c. shredded Cheddar cheese

Unroll crescent roll dough; press into a greased 9" round baking pan, pinching seams closed. Bake at 350 degrees for 10 minutes; set aside. Add beef, seasoning and tomato sauce to a 12" skillet; heat through, about 7 minutes. Pour into crust; sprinkle cheese on top. Bake for 10 to 15 minutes. Set aside 5 minutes before serving. Serves 4.

mains

Summer Sausage

Naomi Cooper
Delaware, OH

*Add a side of redskin potatoes and a tossed salad
for a fresh summery meal.*

2 lbs. ground beef
2 T. pickling salt
1 t. liquid smoke

1/8 t. garlic powder
1/4 c. water

Combine ingredients together; add 1/4 cup water and mix well. Divide
and shape into 4 loaves; wrap individually in plastic wrap and
refrigerate for 24 hours. Remove plastic wrap; arrange loaves on a
broiler pan. Bake at 300 degrees for 1-1/2 hours. Makes 4 servings.

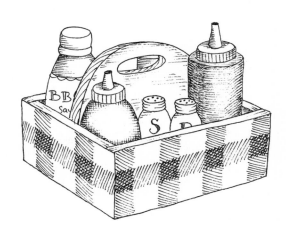

Turn unfinished wooden boxes into vacation keepsakes.
Whitewash on all sides and glue pretty shells on top to remember
the beach even when miles and seasons away!

Summer

Crispy Taco Chicken

Jinnielynn Howell
Wentzville, MO

This recipe was given to me by my best friend, Lisa...everyone should have a best friend like her!

3/4 c. bread crumbs
1-1/4 oz. pkg. taco seasoning
   mix

4 boneless, skinless chicken
   breasts
1/2 c. mayonnaise

Combine bread crumbs and taco seasoning; set aside. Spread chicken with mayonnaise; coat with bread crumb mixture. Arrange on an aluminum foil-lined baking sheet; bake at 425 degrees for 20 minutes or until juices run clear when chicken is pierced with a fork. Makes 4 servings.

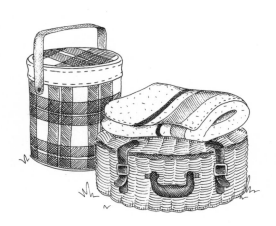

Jelly jars make lovely lanterns for backyard gatherings! Nestle a tea light inside and hang with wire from tree branches or fenceposts. Look for citronella candles to keep mosquitoes away.

Double-Cheese Burritos

Jan O'Brien
Oakton, VA

These roll-ups are so quick & easy...you'll love 'em!

4 to 5 boneless, skinless chicken
  breasts, cooked and
  shredded
8-oz. pkg. cream cheese,
  softened

12-oz. jar salsa, divided
8 10-inch flour tortillas
8-oz. pkg. pasteurized process
  cheese spread, cubed

Stir chicken, cream cheese and one cup salsa together; mix well.
Spoon mixture down the center of each tortilla; roll up and place
seam-side down in an ungreased 13"x9" baking pan. Set aside. Melt
cheese cubes in a heavy saucepan; pour over tortillas. Spread with
remaining salsa; bake at 350 degrees for 30 minutes. Makes
8 servings.

Homemade Flour Tortillas

Jackie Jones
Bozeman, MT

*Roll up burritos or fajitas...they're delicious sprinkled with
cinnamon and sugar too!*

6 c. all-purpose flour
1 t. salt

1 T. baking powder
1-1/4 c. shortening

Combine ingredients together until small crumbs form; gradually add
2 cups hot water. Knead until well blended; divide dough into one to
2-inch balls. Roll out into thin circles; heat until golden in a very hot,
dry skillet. Flip and heat other side; repeat with remaining dough
balls. Makes about 2 dozen.

Cheryl's Lemon Chicken

*Cheryl Hagy
Quarryville, PA*

We love this chicken served over rice.

6 boneless, skinless chicken
   breasts
1/3 c. lemon juice

1/4 c. margarine, melted
1 t. garlic powder
1 t. poultry seasoning

Place chicken in a greased 13"x9" baking pan; set aside. Combine remaining ingredients; pour over chicken. Bake at 350 degrees for one hour. Serves 4 to 6.

Russian Chicken

*Betty Richer
Grand Junction, CO*

Not the same old chicken...everyone will ask what's in it!

3 to 4 lbs. chicken
1/4 c. mayonnaise
1-1/2 oz. pkg. onion soup mix

1/2 c. Russian dressing
1 c. apricot pineapple preserves

Arrange chicken in an ungreased 13"x9" baking pan; set aside. Mix remaining ingredients; spread over chicken. Bake at 350 degrees for 1-1/4 hours. Serves 4.

Roll up brightly colored dish towels and tie with a ribbon or some raffia. Place in a basket for a quick & easy housewarming or shower gift!

mains

Lemon Herb & Garlic Shrimp

Tyson Ann Trecannelli
Fishing Creek, MD

*I keep the ingredients on hand needed to whip up this meal...great
for unexpected company.*

1 to 2 cloves garlic, minced
1/8 c. olive oil
4 to 6 T. butter

1-lb. pkg. frozen, cooked shrimp
1.1-oz. pkg. lemon herb soup
  mix

Sauté garlic in olive oil and butter for 2 minutes; add shrimp. Simmer
until shrimp thaws; stir often. Dissolve soup seasoning mix in one cup
warm water; pour over shrimp mixture. Simmer until warmed through,
about 20 minutes. Makes 6 to 8 servings.

Vintage milk bottles make clever last-minute vases. Fill with small
bouquets of cut flowers from the garden and line up a few
down the center of the table.

Easy-As-1-2-3 Chicken Bake

Barbara Bower
Orrville, OH

Serve with steamed broccoli or asparagus.

3/4 c. corn flake cereal, crushed
3/4 c. grated Parmesan cheese
1-oz. pkg. Italian salad dressing
   mix

8 boneless, skinless chicken
   breasts
1/3 c. margarine, melted

Mix cereal, Parmesan cheese and salad dressing mix together; coat chicken. Place in a single layer in a greased 13"x9" baking pan. Sprinkle remaining crumbs on top; drizzle with butter. Bake at 350 degrees for 45 minutes or until juices run clear when chicken is pierced with a fork. Serves 8.

Sprinkle flower petals, bright green leaves or vintage photos down the center of the table. Lay a chiffon runner over them or any other sheer fabric. Set simple pillar candles on top to secure for a simple and elegant table.

mains

Buttermilk Fried Chicken

Cyndi Little
Whitsett, NC

My daddy made amazing fried chicken, but he passed away when I was 12. It's taken me a long time to make chicken that I feel is almost as good as his.

2-1/2 lbs. chicken	1-1/2 t. salt
1 c. buttermilk	1/2 t. pepper
1 c. all-purpose flour	oil for frying

Combine chicken and buttermilk in a large bowl. Cover and refrigerate for one hour. Meanwhile, combine flour, salt and pepper in a large plastic zipping bag. Drain chicken, discarding buttermilk. Working in batches, add chicken to bag and toss to coat. Shake off excess flour and let chicken rest for 15 minutes. Heat 1/4 inch of oil in a large skillet over medium heat. Fry chicken in oil until golden on all sides. Reduce heat to medium-low; cover and simmer, turning occasionally, for 40 to 45 minutes, until juices run clear. Uncover and cook 5 minutes longer. Serves 4 to 6.

Wire egg baskets can add a nostalgic touch to any room. Pile them high with shiny apples or vintage postcards...look for large square ones to mount on the wall in the bathroom to hold fluffy towels!

Pineapple Dream

Carolynn Smith
Roseville, CA

Cool and refreshing, we love this easy dessert.

2 c. sour cream
1/2 c. sugar
1 t. vanilla extract
12-oz. pkg. vanilla wafers

28-1/2 oz. can crushed
    pineapple, drained
Optional: frozen whipped
    topping, thawed

Combine sour cream, sugar and vanilla together; set aside. Layer vanilla wafers in the bottom of a 13"x9" casserole dish; spread pineapple on top. Add sour cream mixture, spreading evenly; cover and refrigerate for at least 4 hours. Cut into squares to serve; add a dollop of whipped topping before serving, if desired. Makes 12 servings.

Banana Boats

Celia Sanchez
Diamond Bar, CA

Try these over a campfire for a gooey treat!

2 bananas, peeled
1/4 c. semi-sweet chocolate
    chips

1/4 c. mini marshmallows

Split each banana lengthwise, making sure not to cut all the way through the other side. Stuff with chocolate chips and marshmallows; wrap in aluminum foil. Arrange on a baking sheet; bake at 300 degrees for 5 minutes. Serves 2.

desserts

Easy Cherry Cobbler

Krista Starnes
Beaufort, SC

This recipe has been in my family for years! I remember Mom making it for my brother and me...now, I enjoy making it for my family.

1/2 c. butter, melted
2 14-1/2 oz. cans cherry pie
   filling

1 c. self-rising flour
1 c. sugar
1 c. milk

Pour butter in the bottom of a 13"x9" baking pan; spread pie filling on top. In a separate bowl, mix flour, sugar and milk; spoon over pie filling. Bake at 350 degrees for 30 to 45 minutes. Makes 12 to 15 servings.

Cherry Sorbet

Leslie Stimel
Westerville, OH

We like fresh-picked cherries in this recipe.

6 c. semi-sweet cherries, pitted
1/3 c. sugar

juice of one lemon

Place cherries in a mixing bowl; sprinkle sugar evenly over the top. Cover and refrigerate overnight. Pour mixture into a blender; add lemon juice. Purée until smooth; pour into an ice cream maker. Freeze according to manufacturer's instructions. Makes 4 servings.

Summer

Hokey-Pokey Cupcakes

Veva Banks
Neosho, MO

*These scrumptious cupcakes have a surprise
swirl of fruit flavor inside.*

18-1/4 oz. pkg. white cake mix
3-oz. pkg. orange gelatin mix
1 c. boiling water

16-oz. container favorite-flavor
frosting

Prepare cake mix according to package directions, using egg white
version. Spoon into 24 paper-lined muffin cups; bake as directed. Let
cool in pan for 15 minutes. Spray a large fork with non-stick vegetable
spray; pierce cupcakes with fork at 1/4-inch intervals. Place cupcakes
on a paper towel-lined tray; set aside. Add gelatin mix to boiling
water, stirring until dissolved; spoon over cupcakes. Chill cupcakes
for 3 hours. Frost and garnish as desired. Makes 2 dozen.

Don't save pretty cake pedestals for just pastries...pile on fragrant
lemons, limes and green apples for a splash of color.

desserts

Apple Cranberry Popsicles

Jennifer Kirk
Bremerton, WA

Fruity and fun on a hot summer day.

2 c. plain yogurt
2 t. vanilla extract

12-oz. can unsweetened frozen
apple cranberry juice
concentrate, thawed

Mix ingredients together; pour into small paper cups. Insert a plastic spoon into the center of each yogurt cup; freeze overnight. Makes 6.

Butterscotch Haystacks

Tammy Asbill
Whitehouse, TX

Sandwich ice cream between these for a crunchy treat.

2 6-oz. pkgs. butterscotch chips
1 c. cocktail peanuts

3-oz. can chow mein noodles

Melt butterscotch chips in a double boiler; stir in peanuts and noodles. Remove from heat; drop by teaspoonfuls onto wax paper. Set aside to cool until firm. Makes 18.

Rescue an ornate garden gate from a tag sale or auction. Cover any imperfections with matte spray paint and hang on a wall...they're a clever way to display family photos.

summer

Easiest-Ever Cheesecake

Linda Lewanski
Cosby, TN

Friends will think you spent hours on this simple cheesecake.

12-oz. pkg. vanilla wafers,
  crushed
1 c. plus 2 T. sugar, divided
1/2 c. butter, melted

2 8-oz. pkgs. cream cheese,
  softened
12-oz. container frozen whipped
  topping, thawed

Combine vanilla wafers, 2 tablespoons sugar and butter; press into the bottom of a 13"x9" baking pan. In a separate bowl, cream remaining sugar and cream cheese together; fold in whipped topping. Spread over wafer crust; chill until firm. Makes 12 to 15 servings.

Grandma's Shortcake

Mary Freireich
Westerville, OH

Smother with strawberries and cream.

1-1/2 t. salt
3 c. all-purpose flour
4 t. baking powder

2 T. sugar
3/4 c. milk

Mix first 4 ingredients together; gradually add milk. Pat dough into a greased 9"x9" baking pan; bake at 450 degrees for 10 to 12 minutes. Cool; cut into squares to serve. Makes 9 servings.

Love retro style? Search out old packages and make color copies of their whimsical packaging. Mat and place in small frames for a clever grouping.

Spicy Buffalo Chicken Wings, page 174

Brie Kisses, page 177

Party Cheese Ball, page 173

Sausage Balls, page 124

Easy Potato Soup, page 179

Sunday Meeting Tomato Soup, page 19

Chicken & Dumplin' Soup, page 183

Summertime Pasta Salad, page 85

Oven Beef & Noodles, page 201

Pizza Mac & Cheese, page 39

Barbecue Chicken Kabobs, page 89

Buttermilk Fried Chicken, page 103

Cheesy Hashbrowns, page 139

Kale & Potato Casserole, page 207

Mom's Meat Loaf, page 195

Maple-Glazed Carrots, page 30

Grandma's Buttery Mashed Potatoes, page 31

Anytime Cheesy Biscuits, page 7

No-Fuss Tomato Sauce, page 87

Strawberry-Watermelon
Slush, page 13

Hokey-Pokey Cupcakes, page 106

Chocolate-Cherry Crunch, page 49

From-Scratch Brownies, page 211

Cinnamon Poached Pears, page 163

desserts

Lemon Bars

Laura Strausberger
Roswell, GA

Dust with powdered sugar, if you like.

1 c. chilled butter
2 c. all-purpose flour
4 eggs

2 c. sugar
1/4 c. lemon juice

Cut butter into flour until crumbly; press into an ungreased 13"x9" baking pan. Bake at 350 degrees for 30 minutes; set aside to cool. Blend eggs, sugar and lemon juice together; pour over crust. Bake at 325 degrees for 25 minutes; cool. Cut into squares. Makes 24 servings.

Use vintage mini cake molds to make charming candles. Use melted colored wax or a mixture of white wax and colored candies... a birthday candle in the center makes an easy wick. Perfect last-minute gifts for birthdays, holidays or anytime!

summer

Scrumptious Strawberry Pie

Norma Barrett
Sallisaw, OK

The best of summer desserts!

14-oz. can sweetened condensed
  milk
5 T. lemon juice
12-oz. container frozen whipped
  topping, thawed

1 qt. strawberries, hulled and
  sliced
9-inch pie crust, baked

Blend milk and lemon juice together until thick; fold in whipped
topping. Add strawberries; stir gently. Spread into pie crust; refrigerate
for 3 to 4 hours. Makes 8 servings.

Layer colorful jellybeans or candy-coated chocolates in a glass vase
for a sweet surprise for a friend or co-worker...don't
forget to tie with a ribbon!

desserts

Frozen Watermelon Slices

Vickie

Enjoy them at the picnic table on a sunny day.

1 honeydew melon
1 gal. raspberry sherbet

chocolate chips

Refrigerate melon for at least 2 hours so that it is well chilled; slice in half. Scoop out seeds; pack each center with raspberry sherbet. Slice each half into 4 wedges; press chocolate chips into the sherbet along the bottom edges to look like seeds. Serve immediately. Makes 8 servings.

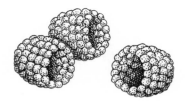

Rhubarb Cobbler

Nola Stephenson
Longview, WA

Top with vanilla ice cream!

5 c. rhubarb, chopped
1 c. sugar
3-oz. pkg. strawberry gelatin
   mix

3 c. mini marshmallows
18-1/4 oz. pkg. yellow cake mix

Place rhubarb in an ungreased 13"x9" baking pan; set aside. Mix sugar and gelatin mix together; sprinkle over rhubarb. Add marshmallows; set aside. Mix cake as directed on package; pour over fruit. Bake at 350 degrees for one hour. Makes 15 servings.

Easy Key Lime Pie

Paula Eggleston
Knoxville, TN

Spread some extra whipped topping on top!

6-oz. can frozen limeade
    concentrate, thawed
14-oz. can sweetened condensed
    milk

9-oz. container frozen whipped
    topping, thawed
9-inch graham cracker pie crust

Combine limeade, milk and whipped topping in a large mixing bowl; mix well. Pour into pie crust; freeze until firm, about 3 to 4 hours. Serves 8.

Vintage cotton napkins look so pretty hung across a curtain rod in the kitchen...look for mismatched sets in gingham, polka dot and old-fashioned ticking.

Autumn

By all these lovely tokens
September days are here,
With summer's best of weather
And autumn's best of cheer.
- Helen Hunt Jackson

autumn

Pepperoni Bread ▶

Jennifer Carr
Pearisburg, VA

Serve warm pizza sauce on the side for dipping!

1 loaf frozen bread dough, thawed	4-oz. pkg. sliced pepperoni 1 c. shredded mozzarella cheese

Roll out bread dough into a 15"x10" rectangle; arrange pepperoni slices and cheese on top. Roll up lengthwise; secure closed with toothpicks. Place on a greased baking sheet; bake at 325 degrees for 25 to 30 minutes. Slice to serve. Makes 12 servings.

Paint silly Jack-'O-Lantern faces on treat bags or kraft paper bags. Tie with a green ribbon for the stem and fill with old-fashioned peanut butter kisses...yum!

appetizers

Jalapeño Cheese Log

Pam Addison
Atkinson, NE

Bring out baskets of crackers for this treat.

16-oz. pkg. pasteurized process
   cheese spread
8-oz. pkg. cream cheese,
   softened

4-oz. can jalapeño peppers,
   drained and chopped
2-1/4 oz. can sliced black olives,
   drained

Place cheese spread between 2 pieces of wax paper and roll out to
1/4-inch thick rectangle; spread with cream cheese. Sprinkle with
peppers and olives; roll up into a log. Wrap in plastic wrap; refrigerate
until serving. Serves 8 to 10.

Warm Mexicali Dip

Tonya Lewis
Crothersville, IN

Serve with crunchy chips.

1 lb. ground beef
1 lb. ground sausage
10-3/4 oz. can cream of
   mushroom soup

4-oz. can diced green chiles,
   drained
8-oz. pkg. pasteurized process
   cheese spread, cubed

Brown ground beef and sausage together; drain. Place in a slow
cooker; stir in remaining ingredients. Heat on low setting until cheese
melts, stirring occasionally. Serves 8 to 10.

For a Thanksgiving arrangement, fill a glass vase with plump
kumquats to anchor flower stems...scatter
fall foliage on the table too!

autumn

Caramel Apple Dip

Jennifer Hatridge
Georgetown, ME

*Fill up a bowl with sliced green, red and yellow apples
and dip away!*

8-oz. pkg. cream cheese,
   softened

1 c. brown sugar, packed
1 t. vanilla extract

Cream ingredients together; cover and refrigerate overnight. Serve
cold. Makes about 2 cups.

Spend a day at the apple orchard with the family and surprise a
neighbor with a bushel basket full of red, gold and green apples.
Add a batch of Caramel Apple Dip for a sweet treat!

appetizers

Raspberry-Cheese Dip

Shelly Lowry
Pearland, TX

The perfect combination of savory and sweet.

2 c. shredded sharp Cheddar
  cheese
2 c. shredded mild Cheddar
  cheese

1 c. mayonnaise
2 green onions, chopped
12-oz. jar raspberry preserves

Mix first 4 ingredients together; spread into a 10" springform pan. Refrigerate for at least 24 hours; remove from pan and place on a serving plate. Spread preserves over the top. Makes about 5 cups.

Lemon Yogurt Fruit Dip

Jamie Rose
Lake Nebagamon, WI

Dip pineapple, strawberries, cantaloupe, apples
or your favorite fruit.

3-1/2 oz. pkg. instant vanilla
  pudding mix
1 c. lemon yogurt

1 c. sour cream
1 T. lemon juice

Whisk ingredients together; cover and chill until serving. Makes 2 cups.

Kitchen gifts are welcome for any occasion! Tie up a few long cinnamon sticks or a bundle of dried herbs with a bow or fill a small bag with personalized herb blends from the garden.

autumn

Ham & Cheese Roll-Ups

Wendy Donovan
Federalsburg, MD

A crispy variation on this finger-food favorite.

1 lb. cooked ham, thinly sliced
1 lb. Swiss cheese, thinly sliced
1/2 c. butter, melted

1 c. bread crumbs
1 c. grated Parmesan cheese

Roll up one ham slice and one cheese slice together; secure with a toothpick. Dip in butter, bread crumbs and then Parmesan cheese. Arrange on an ungreased baking sheet; repeat with remaining ham and cheese slices. Bake at 350 degrees for 10 to 15 minutes. Makes about 24.

Frame fall's foliage in a wooden frame and hang in small groups. Dip leaves in glycerine, let dry and glue onto heavy white paper... stamp a label underneath, if desired.

appetizers

Salami-Cheese Rolls

Julie Wilson
Ventura, CA

*Guests will eat these up before you have time
to make a second batch!*

8-oz. pkg. cream cheese,   1 lb. salami, thinly sliced
   softened

Spread cream cheese on each slice of salami; roll up and secure with a
toothpick. Chill until firm; slice each into quarters. Makes 48.

Chili-Cheese Dip

Beth Jocolano
Penfield, NY

Serve with crispy tortilla chips!

8-oz. pkg. cream cheese,   2 c. shredded Cheddar cheese
   softened
10-1/2 oz. can chili without
   beans

Spread cream cheese in the bottom of an ungreased 13"x9" baking
pan; spread chili on top. Sprinkle with cheese. Bake at 350 degrees for
20 minutes. Serves 10.

Fill a Shaker-style box
with homemade goodies and
pass on to a dear friend. Use
paints or rubber stamps to
personalize the box and tie
it all up with raffia.

autumn

Chipped Beef Spread

Mandy Van Camp
Toledo, OH

Yummy with crackers and veggies too!

2-1/2 oz. pkg. dried, chipped
   beef, chopped
8-oz. pkg. cream cheese,
   softened

1 T. mayonnaise
2 scallions, chopped

Mix ingredients together in a serving dish; cover with plastic wrap and refrigerate overnight. Makes about 1-1/2 cups.

Add a lovely touch of nature to white pillar candles. Lay the candle on its side and place colorful autumn leaves on the surface. Working on newspaper, spoon melted wax over the leaves until they are covered. Allow melted wax to cool and smooth surface with the back of a spoon.

appetizers

Reuben Bread Bowl Dip

Mary Hastings
Gurnee, IL

All the taste of the classic sandwich in this cheesy dip.

2 round loaves rye bread
8-oz. pkg. cream cheese,
   softened

4-oz. pkg. shredded mozzarella
   cheese
2 2-1/2 oz. pkgs. dried, chipped
   beef, diced

Hollow out the center of one loaf of bread; set aside. Cube removed and remaining loaf of bread; set aside. Mix cream cheese and mozzarella cheese together; fold in chipped beef. Spoon into bread center; bake at 350 degrees for 1-1/4 hours. Serve warm on a serving platter surrounded with bread cubes. Serves 8 to 10.

For a Halloween buffet table, nestle a few Jack-'O-Lanterns
of different sizes topped with bewitching hats
on a handful of raffia for hair.

autumn

Sweet Onion Spread

Lisa Woynowski
Crest Hill, IL

Serve warm on crusty baguette slices.

2 sweet onions, minced
1-1/2 c. shredded Parmesan
   cheese, divided

1 c. mayonnaise
1 c. sour cream
1 T. dill weed, divided

Blend onions, one cup Parmesan cheese, mayonnaise, sour cream and 2-1/2 teaspoons dill weed together until well blended; spoon mixture into 2 ungreased 9" glass pie pans. Sprinkle with remaining cheese and dill weed; bake at 325 degrees for 40 to 45 minutes or until golden. Serve warm. Serves 12.

Hand out tricks & treats in Halloween style! Rubber stamp leaves, pumpkins or little black cats onto kraft paper bags and fill with wrapped candies of all kinds. So easy!

122

appetizers

Grandma Paris' Bambinis

Kristin Santangelo
Jersey City, NJ

*My grandma and mom entered this recipe in the Rochester, NY
Cook-Off and won first prize! They're 2 of the best cooks
in the world and have both taught me so much.*

1 c. ricotta cheese
1/2 c. shredded mozzarella
   cheese
1/4 c. grated Parmesan cheese

10-oz. tube refrigerated large
   flaky biscuits
20 thin slices pepperoni

Combine cheeses in a mixing bowl; set aside. Halve each biscuit
horizontally; gently shape into a 4"x2-1/2" oval. Place one pepperoni
slice and one tablespoon cheese mixture in the upper half of each oval;
fold dough up and over filling, pinching closed. Repeat with remaining
ingredients. Arrange on a lightly greased baking sheet; bake at
350 degrees for 20 minutes. Makes 20.

Look for vintage pie plates at the flea market...filled with votives
and ornamental gourds, they'll add a warm glow to fall festivities.

autumn

Sausage Balls

Laura Strausberger
Roswell, GA

Double the recipe or make 'em minis for a crowd.

1 lb. ground sausage
2 c. biscuit baking mix

12-oz. pkg. shredded Cheddar
   cheese

Combine ingredients together; shape into one-inch balls. Arrange on an ungreased baking sheet; bake at 425 degrees for 12 to 15 minutes. Makes about 5 dozen.

Cheese Bread Bites

Nola Laflin
Coral Springs, FL

I like simple and easy make-ahead recipes. This is a favorite of my grandchildren and family. When they tell me when they're flying into Florida, I start making and storing these right away!

1 loaf French bread, crusts
   trimmed
1 c. butter
1/2 lb. sharp Cheddar cheese,
   cubed

2 3-oz. pkgs. cream cheese,
   softened
4 egg whites, stiffly beaten

Cube bread; set aside. Melt butter and cheeses in a double boiler over low heat, stirring often. Remove from heat; fold in egg whites. Dip bread cubes into cheese mixture; set on greased baking sheets. Place in freezer until frozen; remove from baking sheets and store in plastic zipping bags in the freezer. To serve, bake frozen bites at 400 degrees for 12 minutes on greased baking sheets. Serves 8 to 10.

Set a pail of mini pumpkins on the front porch for a cheery welcome to trick-or-treaters!

appetizers

Baked Parmesan Dip

*Rose Salinas
Whigham, GA*

Use corn chips as scoops!

2 8-oz. pkgs. cream cheese,
   softened
1/2 c. mayonnaise

2 c. grated Parmesan cheese
2/3 c. onions, diced

Mix ingredients together; spread into an ungreased 8"x8" baking
pan. Bake at 400 degrees for 20 minutes or until golden and bubbly.
Serves 10.

Welcome Autumn with a wreath on the front door! Decorate a
purchased wreath form with clusters of berries, ornamental
grasses and other fall finds. Simply attach the
fall finds with wire or hot glue.

autumn

Cheesy Onion Muffins

Melinda Einan
Wrightstown, WI

Use 12 to 15 mini English muffins for a bite-size variation.

3-1/2 c. shredded Cheddar
    cheese
1/4 c. onion, minced

1/4 c. mayonnaise-type salad
    dressing
6 to 8 English muffins, split

Mix cheese, onion and salad dressing together; spread over muffin halves. Arrange on a broiler pan; broil until golden. Slice in half to serve. Makes 12 to 16 servings.

Gold and silver metallic felt-tip pens make placecards easy...write guests' names on mini pumpkins, pretty leaves or individual votive holders.

soups & breads

Old-Fashioned Lima Bean Soup

Nancy Wise
Little Rock, AR

A hearty recipe that you don't have to stew over!

3-1/2 to 4 lbs. chicken
1-lb. pkg. dried lima beans
2 carrots, sliced

1 stalk celery, sliced
1 onion, chopped

Cover chicken with water in a large stockpot; gently boil for one hour. Lower heat; add beans, carrots, celery and onion. Simmer until beans are tender, about 2 hours. Remove chicken; bone and chop. Return chicken to stockpot; heat through. Serves 6 to 8.

Bunches of bittersweet tucked into a grapevine wreath will welcome autumn guests at the front door.

autumn

Cornbread Corn Casserole

Tina Knotts
Cable, OH

My "must bring" dish to every family gathering.

8-1/2 oz. pkg. corn muffin mix
2 15-oz. cans creamed corn
1 egg

1/3 c. butter, melted
3/4 c. sour cream

Combine ingredients together; pour into a greased 13"x9" baking pan. Bake at 375 degrees for 35 to 45 minutes. Makes 8 to 10 servings.

An old-fashioned stoneware butter crock makes a festive fall centerpiece when filled with Indian corn and dried flowers.

soups & breads

Tex-Mex Chili

Dawn Lang
West Liberty, OH

*Our favorite toppings are shredded Cheddar cheese
and chopped jalapeños.*

1 lb. ground beef, browned
15-oz. can hot chili beans
15-1/2 oz. can kidney beans

12-oz. jar salsa
1-1/4 oz. pkg. chili seasoning
mix

Combine all the ingredients together in a large stockpot; add 1/2 to
one cup water. Bring to a boil over medium heat; reduce heat and
simmer for 10 to 15 minutes. Serves 4.

Cowboy Beef Stew

JoAngela Vassey
Cherry Hill, NJ

Yeehaw! Dinner's done!

5 to 6 potatoes, peeled and diced
2 carrots, peeled and thinly
    sliced

1 lb. ground beef
1 T. all-purpose flour
8-oz. can tomato sauce

Place potatoes and carrots in a saucepan; add enough water to cover
vegetables by an inch. Boil gently until tender, about 30 minutes; set
aside. Shape ground beef into one-inch meatballs; brown in a
12" skillet. Add undrained vegetable mixture; heat for 5 minutes and
set aside. Whisk flour and 1/2 cup water together in a small mixing
bowl; pour in tomato sauce. Stir into beef mixture; cover and simmer
until thickened, about 15 minutes. Serves 4.

autumn

Savory Muffins

Carla McRorie
Kannapolis, NC

Even my husband can make these hearty muffins.

1 c. self-rising flour
1 t. baking powder

1/2 c. milk
2 T. mayonnaise

Combine ingredients together; fill greased or paper-lined muffin tins
2/3 full with batter. Bake at 400 degrees until golden, about
20 minutes. Makes 6.

Keep an eye out for vintage cake stands at flea markets and
auctions. Not just for cakes and pastries anymore, try them
out as centerpieces holding candles or fresh fruit.

soups & breads

Vegetable-Cheese Chowder

Kathy Grashoff
Fort Wayne, IN

For variety, use Swiss or smoked Gouda cheese.

16-oz. pkg. frozen broccoli,
    cauliflower and carrot mix
2 c. milk, divided

1/3 c. all-purpose flour
14-1/2 oz. can chicken broth
1 c. Gouda cheese, shredded

Prepare vegetables according to package directions; do not drain. Whisk 2/3 cup milk and flour together; mix well. Pour into vegetables; stir in remaining milk and chicken broth. Heat, stirring often, until thickened and bubbly; heat one minute more. Reduce heat to low; stir in Gouda cheese until melted. Makes 4 servings.

Homestyle Goulash

Price Brister
Alexandria, LA

Serve with warm garlic bread sticks and a tossed salad.

1-1/2 to 2 lbs. ground beef
1 onion, diced
4 cloves garlic, minced
15-1/2 oz. can kidney beans

2 14-3/4 oz. cans spaghetti with
    tomato and cheese sauce

Sauté ground beef and onion until browned; drain. Add garlic; sauté for 5 minutes. Reduce heat; stir in beans and spaghetti. Simmer, covered, for 25 minutes. Serves 4 to 6.

Everyone must take time to sit and
watch the leaves turn.
- Elizabeth Lawrence

Lemony Poppy Seed Bread

Vicki Moats
Wyoming, IL

Mini loaves wrapped in pretty plastic wrap make
welcome gifts any time of year!

18-1/4 oz. pkg. lemon cake mix
3-1/2 oz. pkg. instant lemon
   pudding mix

4 eggs
1/2 c. oil
1 to 2 t. poppy seed

Blend ingredients together; add one cup water, mixing well. Pour into two, 8"x4" greased and floured loaf pans; bake at 350 degrees for 50 to 60 minutes. Makes 16 servings.

Make whimsical "topiaries" from small pumpkins and colorful gourds. Use a rustic branch to hold them up in a terra cotta pot!

soups & breads

Easy Italian Wedding Soup

Debby Horton
Cincinnati, OH

We sprinkle each serving with grated Parmesan cheese.

2 14-1/2 oz. cans chicken broth
1 c. medium shell pasta,
    uncooked
16 frozen meatballs, cooked

2 c. spinach leaves, finely
    shredded
8-oz. can pizza sauce

Bring broth and one cup water to a boil in a large saucepan; add pasta
and meatballs. Return to a boil; heat until pasta is done, about 7 to
9 minutes. Do not drain. Reduce heat; stir in spinach and pizza sauce.
Heat thoroughly, about one to 2 minutes. Makes 4 servings.

Dress up a pillar candle in seconds! Press whole cloves into the
candle in the shape of a leaf, tree or star. Surround with
fall foliage for a quick & easy centerpiece.

autumn

Busy-Day Vegetable Soup

Cindy Norred
Roanoke, AL

Perfect when you need a hot meal in a hurry!

1 lb. ground beef, browned
2 28-oz. cans whole tomatoes,
   chopped

2 15-oz. cans mixed vegetables
3 bay leaves
1 onion, sliced

Mix ingredients together in a large stockpot; stir to mix well. Bring to a boil; reduce heat and simmer for 20 to 25 minutes. Discard bay leaves before serving. Makes 6 servings.

Press pretty autumn leaves between 2 sheets of wax paper and place a cloth on top. Using a warm iron, press and then let cool. Trim the edges of the wax paper with pinking shears. Use as a placemat or cut out individual leaves, add a ribbon and hang in a sunny window!

soups & breads

Miner's Stew

Delores Harty
Bridgeville, PA

Grandma used to make this recipe when I was small...the recipe was handed down to me and it's just as yummy today as it was back then.

1 lb. ground beef
8 potatoes, peeled and sliced
1 onion, sliced

8-oz. can tomato sauce
salt and pepper to taste

Layer beef, potatoes and onions in an ungreased 2-quart casserole dish; set aside. Mix tomato sauce and one canful water together; pour over casserole. Salt and pepper to taste. Bake, covered, at 350 degrees until potatoes are tender, about 1-1/2 hours. Serves 4.

Beans & More Soup

Sharon Lundberg
Longwood, FL

White rice is tasty on the side or even stirred into the soup!

2 14-1/2 oz. cans chicken broth
14-oz. can stewed tomatoes with
   Italian seasonings
2 16-oz. cans navy beans,
   rinsed and drained

16-oz. pkg. frozen mixed
   vegetables, partially thawed
1/2 t. garlic powder

Combine ingredients in a large stockpot; heat until boiling. Reduce heat; simmer until heated through. Serves 4.

Fill an oversized mug with some flavored tea bags and a new tea ball...give along with a good book for an afternoon of relaxation.

Apple-Celery Salad

Wendy Lee Paffenroth
Pine Island, NY

Crunchy and oh-so yummy!

1 c. celery, diced
1 c. apples, cored and diced
1/2 c. chopped walnuts or
    pecans

3/4 c. mayonnaise
salt to taste

Gently fold ingredients together in a serving bowl; cover and chill until serving. Serves 4.

Candy Bar-Apple Salad

Denise Pepin
Chicago, IL

Tastes just like a caramel apple!

8-oz. pkg. cream cheese,
    softened
1/2 c. brown sugar, packed
4 to 6 Granny Smith apples,
    cored, peeled and chopped

6 2.16-oz. caramel peanut
    candy bars, chopped
8-oz. container frozen whipped
    topping, thawed

Blend cream cheese and brown sugar together; fold in apples and candy bars. Gently stir in whipped topping. Makes 8 servings.

No harvest season is complete without a trip to the pumpkin patch!
Pick your own pumpkins, gourds and squash.
Choose a cool afternoon and enjoy!

Salads & Sides

Sweet Potato-Apple Bake

Joann Sklarsky
Johnstown, PA

Just right alongside roasted turkey.

29-oz. can sweet potatoes
21-oz. can apple pie filling

16-oz. can whole berry
   cranberry sauce

Carefully fold ingredients together; spread into a buttered 2-quart casserole dish. Bake at 350 degrees until potatoes are heated, about 30 to 45 minutes. Serves 4.

Chunky Applesauce

Kelly Hall
Columbus, OH

Easier than opening up a can!

2 c. apples, cored, peeled
   and cubed

1/2 c. sugar
1/2 t. cinnamon

Mix ingredients together in a microwave-safe bowl; add 1/4 cup water, stirring gently. Cover and microwave for 7 minutes; stir every one to 2 minutes. Serves 2.

An easy harvest centerpiece...fill a bowl with bright green apples then tuck a few cut mums in harvest colors between the apples and set on the table.

autumn

Potato-Beef Casserole

Nancy Garrison
Jerseyville, IL

Hearty and tummy-warming!

5 potatoes, peeled and diced
1 onion, diced
1/2 lb. ground beef, browned

10-3/4 oz. can cream of
mushroom soup

Place potatoes and onion in an ungreased 13"x9" baking pan; set aside. Mix ground beef and soup together; add one cup water. Spread over potatoes; bake at 350 degrees for one hour. Serves 6.

Plant pots of mums and other fall favorites in old-fashioned sap buckets or galvanized pails. Placed by the front door, they'll provide a warm welcome.

Salads & Sides

Upside-Down Baked Potatoes

Shaaron Jones
Bloomfield, MO

These cheesy potatoes are just right for chilly afternoons.

4 T. margarine, melted
2 T. grated Parmesan cheese

4 to 6 potatoes, cut in half
   lengthwise

Coat bottom of a 13"x9" baking pan with margarine; sprinkle cheese on top. Place potatoes cut-side down in pan; bake at 400 degrees for 30 to 40 minutes. Serves 4 to 6.

Cheesy Hashbrowns

Joanne McDonald
British Columbia, Canada

Top with French fried onions for added crunch, if you'd like.

30-oz. pkg. frozen shredded
   hashbrowns, thawed
2 c. sour cream
2 10-3/4 oz. cans cream of
   mushroom soup

1 onion, chopped
2 to 3 c. shredded Cheddar
   cheese, divided

Combine hashbrowns, sour cream, soup, onion and 2 cups cheese together; mix well. Spread into a lightly buttered 13"x9" baking pan; sprinkle with remaining cheese. Bake at 350 degrees for one hour. Makes 8 to 10 servings.

Rice & Monterey Jack Casserole

Michelle Serrano
Ramona, CA

A yummy side to complement your favorite Mexican dishes.

2 c. sour cream
3 c. prepared rice
2-oz. can diced green chiles

1 c. shredded Monterey Jack
cheese

Combine sour cream, rice and chiles; arrange in layers with cheese in an ungreased 1-1/2 quart casserole dish. Bake at 350 degrees until heated through, about 15 minutes. Makes 6 servings.

Remember the littlest trick-or-treater with a photo snapped on the big night! Frame with a mat decorated with Halloween stickers or old-fashioned candy wrappers.

Salads & Sides

Baked French Onion Rice

Tammie McClendon
Guild, TN

This simple, tasty dish requires very little prep time.

1 c. long-cooking rice, uncooked
14-1/2 oz. can beef broth
10-1/2 oz. can French onion
   soup

4-oz. can mushroom stems and
   pieces, drained
1/4 c. margarine

Place rice into an ungreased 2-quart casserole dish; add beef broth, soup and mushroom pieces, stirring well. Dot with margarine; bake at 350 degrees for 50 minutes. Makes 4 servings.

Jordan's Favorite Rice

Vicki Sheets
Hughesville, PA

My son loves any type of rice...he loves this recipe so much,
he often wants to make it himself!

10-3/4 oz. can cream of
   mushroom soup
1/2 c. beef broth
2 c. prepared white rice

1/2 c. frozen peas, thawed,
   cooked and drained
soy sauce to taste

Heat soup and broth in a skillet until boiling; add rice and peas. Reduce heat; simmer until heated through without boiling. Season with soy sauce. Serves 4.

autumn

Tomato-Herb Bake

Linda Newkirk
Central Point, OR

Season to taste with minced garlic, black pepper,
fresh chives or thyme.

5 tomatoes, sliced
9-inch pie crust, baked
1 t. fresh basil, chopped

3/4 c. mayonnaise
1-1/2 c. grated Parmesan cheese

Arrange tomato slices in pie crust; sprinkle with basil and set aside.
Combine mayonnaise and Parmesan cheese; spread over tomatoes.
Bake at 400 degrees for 15 to 20 minutes. Makes 8 servings.

Trim linen napkins for the harvest table with a simple running
stitch along the edge. Choose contrasting embroidery floss or
coordinate with the tablecloth for a personal touch.

Salads & sides

Simple Broccoli Casserole

Margie Schaffner
Altoona, IA

Mix in shredded, cooked chicken if you like.

10-oz. pkg. frozen broccoli,
    thawed
10-3/4 oz. can cream of
    chicken soup

10-3/4 oz. can cream of
    mushroom soup
6-oz. pkg. herb-flavored
    stuffing mix
1/2 c. butter, melted

Place broccoli and soups in a buttered 1-1/2 quart casserole dish; mix well. Toss stuffing with butter in a mixing bowl; add to casserole dish. Stir gently to mix; bake at 350 degrees for 40 to 45 minutes. Makes 4 to 6 servings.

Herbed Corn Bake

Nikole Morningstar
Norfolk, VA

This dish always reminds me of my mom...she loved creating new dishes for our family to enjoy.

1/4 c. butter
1/2 c. cream cheese, softened
1/4 t. onion salt

1 T. fresh chives, chopped
10-oz. pkg. frozen corn, thawed

Melt butter in a heavy saucepan; add cream cheese, onion salt and chives, stirring until cheese melts. Add corn; mix well. Pour into an ungreased 1-1/2 quart casserole dish; cover and bake at 325 degrees until bubbly, about 45 minutes. Serves 4.

autumn

Salisbury Steak Dinner

Sharon Dalton
Jackson, OH

Dollop with sour cream and parsley if desired.

1 T. olive oil
2-lb. pkg. cubed steak
29-oz. can tomato sauce
14-3/4 oz. can beef gravy

28-oz. pkg. frozen diced
   potatoes with green pepper
   and onion, thawed

Heat olive oil in a skillet over medium heat; brown steak. Drain; place in a large stockpot. Add tomato sauce, gravy and potatoes; bring to a boil. Reduce heat to medium; simmer for 10 minutes or until potatoes are tender. Serves 4.

Add some sparkle to fall festivities! Brush on glue in whimsical swirls or dots on miniature pumpkins and gourds...sprinkle with glitter and line up in a row down the center of the harvest table.

mains

Grandma's Poor Do

Victoria Presnell
Cedar Hill, MO

My mom never shared how this recipe got its name but nevertheless, it's a favorite of my son's and mine.

6 slices bacon
1 stalk celery, chopped
1 onion, chopped

2 15-oz. cans tomato sauce
16-oz. pkg. bowtie pasta, cooked

Sauté bacon, celery and onion until bacon is crisply cooked; pour in tomato sauce. Heat through; gently fold in pasta, stirring well. Serves 4 to 6.

Wanda's Wimpies

Wanda Leuty
Swansen, IL

An easy sloppy joe recipe for busy parents and grandparents.

1-1/2 lbs. ground beef
salt and pepper to taste
10-3/4 oz. can tomato soup

1/2 c. tangy-flavored catsup
6 to 8 sandwich buns

Brown beef in a heavy saucepan; salt and pepper to taste. Add soup and catsup; reduce heat and simmer until thick. Spoon onto buns to serve. Makes 6 to 8 servings.

Tuck Indian corn, bumpy gourds, colorful autumn leaves and bright sunflowers into a Thanksgiving cornucopia for a festive addition to the mantel.

autumn

Baked Spaghetti Ring

Carole Beverage
Grafton, OH

My 3 children love this dish...they always ask for it for their special birthday dinner. Fill center of ring with a bowlful of favorite warmed spaghetti sauce, if desired.

16-oz. pkg. spaghetti, cooked
2 10-oz. pkgs. frozen chopped
   spinach, cooked and drained

1/4 c. onion, chopped
4 eggs, beaten
1-1/3 c. grated Parmesan cheese

Mix ingredients together; pour into a greased Bundt® pan. Cover; bake at 375 degrees for 25 to 30 minutes. Let stand 5 minutes before removing from pan. Serves 4 to 6.

Tomato-Beef Noodle Bake

Carol Wingo
Henderson, TX

Sprinkle on shredded Cheddar cheese before baking for added zest... we love this meal for fall football games!

1 lb. ground beef
1 onion, chopped
10-oz. can tomatoes with chiles
10-3/4 oz. can cream of
   mushroom soup

8-oz. pkg. fine egg noodles,
   cooked

Brown beef and onion in a skillet over medium heat; drain. Add remaining ingredients; place in an ungreased 2-quart casserole dish. Bake at 350 degrees for 20 to 25 minutes, until hot and bubbly. Serves 4.

mains

Hot & Hearty Wraps

Sonya Stocker
Hoxie, AR

No tortillas? Just spoon filling over steamed rice.

1 lb. ground beef, browned
6 eggs, scrambled
16-oz. pkg. frozen broccoli and
    cauliflower flowerets, cooked
    and drained

8 10-inch flour tortillas
salsa to taste

Combine ground beef, eggs and vegetables together in a saucepan; heat through. Spoon into center of tortillas; add salsa. Makes 8 servings.

Fill a wooden salad bowl with dried orange slices, dried apples and fat pine cones for a yummy-smelling addition to the buffet or coffee table.

autumn

Super-Simple Bacon Chicken

Karen Fisher
Cloquet, MN

Way too easy for such a great-tasting dinner!

1 lb. bacon, thinly sliced
6 boneless, skinless chicken
   breasts

salt and pepper to taste

Wrap 2 to 3 slices bacon around each chicken breast; season with salt and pepper. Arrange in an ungreased 13"x9" baking pan; bake at 350 degrees for 30 minutes. Turn chicken and drain drippings; bake 15 to 30 more minutes or until juices run clear when chicken is pierced with a fork. Serves 6.

Surround a simple votive candle with acorns inside a Mason
jar...tie on a raffia bow to welcome Autumn.

mains

Slow-Cooker Chicken Cacciatore

Barbara Spilsbury
Hacienda Heights, CA

Top hot spaghetti with this delicious dish.

6 boneless, skinless chicken
   breasts
28-oz. jar spaghetti sauce

2 green peppers, chopped
1 onion, minced
2 T. minced garlic

Place chicken in a slow cooker; top with remaining ingredients. Cover; cook on low setting for 7 to 9 hours. Serves 6.

Garlic Chicken

Nicole Shira
New Baltimore, MI

Serve with steamed broccoli and mashed potatoes.

4 cloves garlic, chopped
1/4 c. olive oil
1/2 c. garlic herb Parmesan
   cheese

1/2 c. seasoned bread crumbs
4 boneless, skinless chicken
   breasts

Mix garlic with olive oil; place in a microwave-safe bowl. Microwave on high for 3 minutes; set aside. Combine Parmesan cheese and bread crumbs together; place in a shallow dish. Dip chicken in garlic mixture; coat with bread crumb mixture. Place in an ungreased 13"x9" baking pan; bake at 425 degrees for 35 minutes or until juices run clear when chicken is pierced with a fork. Serves 4.

Make handmade gifts even more special with clever tags. Make a pumpkin from a fat button or cut the tag into the shape of a leaf!

autumn

Pecan Chicken

Linda Wiist
Duluth, GA

Garnish with a pecan half, if desired.

4 boneless, skinless chicken
    breasts
2 T. honey

2 T. Dijon mustard
2 T. ground pecans

Place chicken between 2 sheets of heavy-duty plastic wrap; flatten
to 1/4-inch thickness using a rolling pin. Set aside. Mix honey and
mustard together; spread over chicken. Coat chicken with pecans;
arrange in a lightly greased 13"x9" baking pan. Bake at 350 degrees
for 15 to 18 minutes. Makes 4 servings.

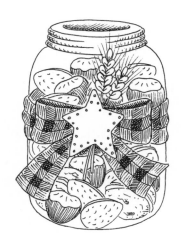

Fill up a simple glass jar with an assortment of hazelnuts, almonds,
pecans and walnuts in their shells. Tie with a homespun
ribbon for an easy hostess gift.

Chicken Pot Pie

Angela Brown
Walnut Ridge, AR

Season to taste before topping with biscuits.

2 c. chicken, cooked and
  chopped
15-oz. can mixed vegetables,
  drained

2 10-3/4 oz. cans cream of
  chicken soup
1 c. milk
10-oz. tube refrigerated biscuits

Combine first 4 ingredients together; place in an ungreased 3-quart casserole dish. Bake at 400 degrees for 20 minutes. While baking, slice biscuits into quarters; set aside. Remove dish from oven and stir. Arrange biscuit pieces on top of hot chicken mixture; bake until golden about 15 minutes. Makes 6 servings.

Chicken & Rice Casserole

Joyce Huber
Santa Clara, CA

This dish is very rich and makes great leftovers too!

4 boneless, skinless chicken
  breasts, cooked and
  shredded
3 10-3/4 oz. cans cream of
  chicken soup

6 c. cooked rice
3 c. mayonnaise
8 eggs, hard-boiled, peeled,
  chopped and divided

Mix all ingredients except for 2 eggs in an ungreased 13"x9" baking pan; sprinkle with remaining eggs. Bake at 325 degrees for 30 minutes or until top is golden. Serve hot or cold. Serves 4 to 6.

autumn

Beef & Noodle Skillet

Angie Dixon
Pevely, MO

Hearty and zesty to warm your tummy.

1 lb. ground beef, browned
2 10-1/2 oz. cans beef broth
8-oz. pkg. elbow macaroni

16-oz. pkg. pasteurized process
   cheese spread, cubed
1 c. salsa

Place beef in a 12" skillet; add broth. Heat to boiling; stir in macaroni.
Boil until macaroni is tender; reduce heat and mix in cheese and salsa.
Heat through, stirring occasionally. Serves 4.

Sweet & Savory Roast

Patsy Stembridge
Wylliesburg, VA

Makes a delicious gravy to spoon over mashed potatoes.

12-oz. can cola
10-3/4 oz. can cream of
   mushroom soup

3 to 4-lb. boneless chuck roast
2 onions, thinly sliced

Combine cola and soup together; set aside. Place roast in a roasting
pan; pour soup mixture on top. Add onions; cover and bake at
325 degrees for 2-1/2 to 3 hours. Serves 8 to 10.

Country Sausage & Potatoes

Crystal Branstrom
Russell, PA

Any veggies work well...we like it with broccoli, carrots and cauliflower.

1-lb. pkg. Kielbasa, chopped
1 onion, chopped
1 T. oil

9-oz. pkg. au gratin potato mix
8-oz. pkg. frozen mixed
    vegetables

Brown Kielbasa and onion in oil for about 5 minutes; stir in potatoes, sauce mix and 2-1/2 cups hot water. Heat to boiling; reduce heat and simmer, covered, for 10 minutes, stirring occasionally. Add frozen vegetables; simmer until vegetables are tender. Makes 4 servings.

Display mini pumpkins and gourds in a whole new way...use them in a wide-mouth jar to secure bittersweet, cattails and dried autumn grasses for a nothing-to-it centerpiece!

autumn

Salsa Lasagna

Lori Lybarger
Gambier, OH

Serve with sour cream and chopped green onions.

16-oz. can refried beans
1 c. salsa
9 lasagna noodles, cooked and
    divided

1 c. cottage cheese, divided
1-1/2 c. shredded Cheddar
    cheese, divided

Combine refried beans and salsa in a small saucepan; heat until warmed, stirring well. Spread 2 tablespoons salsa mixture in the bottom of an ungreased 8"x8" baking pan; arrange 3 noodles on top. Layer with half the remaining salsa mixture, half the cottage cheese and then 1/2 cup Cheddar cheese. Repeat layers beginning with the noodles; top with remaining noodles and Cheddar cheese. Bake at 350 degrees until bubbly, about 30 minutes. Makes 9 servings.

Line up these clever candles on the mantel or dining room table.
Just hollow out a few mini pumpkins and pop a
tea light inside. So simple!

mains

Corned Beef Casserole

Sherri Starman
Des Moines, IA

Very quick to put together...and gone in a flash!

7-1/4 oz. pkg. macaroni &
    cheese
12-oz. can corned beef
10-3/4 oz. can cream of
    celery soup

10-3/4 oz. can cream of
    chicken soup
1/4 to 1/2 c. milk

Boil macaroni until tender; drain. Stir in beef and soups; mix well. Add half the cheese packet from the box of macaroni and cheese; stir in milk. Pour into an ungreased 2-quart casserole dish; sprinkle remaining cheese on top. Bake at 350 degrees for one hour. Serves 4.

Pizza Burgers

June Gravitte
Renfrew, PA

A great tailgating dinner and freezes well too.

1 lb. ground beef, browned
1 lb. chipped ham, chopped
15-oz. can pizza sauce

16-oz. pkg. sharp American
    cheese slices, cubed
8 to 10 onion sandwich buns

Combine beef, ham and pizza sauce together in a saucepan; heat on low until warmed through. Stir in cheese until melted; spoon onto buns to serve. Makes 8 to 10.

autumn

Company Chicken

Jo Anne Hayon
Sheboygan, WI

Serve up with a side of rice and sautéed mushrooms.

8 slices Canadian bacon
4 boneless, skinless chicken
    breasts
10-3/4 oz. can cream of
    mushroom soup

1 c. sour cream
Garnish: green onions, chopped

Place bacon in the bottom of greased 13"x9" baking pan; arrange chicken breasts on top. Bake at 350 degrees for 30 minutes. Combine soup and sour cream; spread over the chicken. Continue baking an additional 30 minutes. Garnish with onions. Serves 4.

Look for old-fashioned pottery or stoneware jugs at yard sales, auctions and antique shops. They're charming on the front porch or by the fireplace with a sprig of bittersweet inside.

Chicken & Biscuit Bake

Beverly Krosch
Elmore, MN

Homestyle cooking, this dish is great for potlucks too!

12-oz. tube refrigerated
　buttermilk biscuits
12-1/2 oz. can chicken
1/2 c. milk

10-3/4 oz. can cream of
　chicken soup
4 slices American cheese

Arrange biscuits in a greased 9"x9" baking pan; set aside. Mix chicken, milk and soup together; pour over biscuits. Bake at 350 degrees for 25 minutes; place cheese slices on top and return to oven until cheese melts. Serves 4.

Chix Casserole

Carolyn Green
Shelbyville, TX

This is usually what my kids ask for for dinner!

3/4 c. butter, divided
2 to 3 lbs. chicken
garlic salt and pepper to taste

28-oz. pkg. frozen shredded
　hashbrowns
1 c. shredded Cheddar cheese

Melt 1/2 cup butter; toss with chicken and seasonings. Arrange in an ungreased 13"x9" baking pan; bake at 375 degrees for 20 minutes. Prepare hashbrowns according to package directions; cover each chicken piece with hashbrowns. Place 1/2 teaspoon butter on top of each piece. Bake 30 more minutes; sprinkle with cheese. Bake until cheese is melted and juices run clear when chicken is pierced with a fork, about 10 minutes. Serves 4.

Chocolate-Toffee Bites

Remona Putman
Rockwood, PA

Crunchy and sweet, they'll never guess the secret ingredient.

saltine crackers
1 c. butter
1/2 c. sugar

1 c. chocolate chips
Garnish: chopped walnuts

Line a 15"x10" baking pan with aluminum foil; cover with a single layer of crackers. Melt butter and sugar in a saucepan; boil for 2 minutes. Pour over crackers; bake at 350 degrees for 10 minutes. Sprinkle chocolate chips on top; spread when melted. Add chopped nuts, if desired. Refrigerate until cooled; break into 2-inch squares and store in an airtight container. Makes 25 to 30 servings.

Use pretty glass trifle bowls to hold pillar candles...keep them in place with fall treats like candy corn, popcorn or even dried cranberries.

desserts

Peanut Butter Bars

Angela Sims
Willow Springs, IL

Try with creamy or crunchy peanut butter!

1-1/2 c. graham cracker crumbs
1 c. margarine, melted
16-oz. pkg. powdered sugar
1 c. peanut butter
12-oz. pkg. butterscotch chips

Combine first 4 ingredients together; mix well. Press into the bottom of a 13"x9" baking pan; set aside. Melt butterscotch chips in a double boiler; spread over crumb mixture. Refrigerate; cut into bars when cooled. Makes 24.

Caramel-Marshmallow Delights

Shelley Haverkate
Grandville, MI

Sweet and chewy...what could be better?

14-oz. can sweetened condensed milk
1/2 c. butter
14-oz. pkg. caramels, unwrapped
16-oz. pkg. marshmallows
10-oz. pkg. puffed rice cereal

Combine milk, butter and caramels in a heavy saucepan over medium heat; stir until melted and smooth. Remove from heat; quickly dip marshmallows into mixture and then roll in rice cereal. Arrange on an aluminum foil-lined baking sheet; refrigerate for 30 minutes. Remove from baking sheet; store in an airtight container in the refrigerator. Makes 5 to 6 dozen.

Old-Time Sugar Pie

Brenda Doak
Delaware, OH

A favorite from days gone by.

2 T. all-purpose flour
1 c. sugar
9-inch pie crust

2 c. milk
Optional: cinnamon
1 T. butter

Sprinkle flour and sugar into pie crust; mix gently. Add milk; stir with fingers until smooth. Sprinkle with cinnamon, if desired; dot with butter. Bake at 375 degrees until mixture boils, at least one hour. Cool. Makes 8 servings.

Pumpkin Mallow Pie

Rhea Hristou
Sandy, UT

We love this after a big meal...so light.

1 pt. whipping cream
15-oz. can pumpkin
2 10-oz. pkgs. mini
  marshmallows

1 t. cinnamon
2 9-inch graham cracker pie
  crusts

Whip whipping cream until soft peaks form; set aside. Combine pumpkin, marshmallows and cinnamon in a heavy saucepan; stir over low heat until marshmallows are melted. Cover and chill thoroughly. Blend chilled mixture until fluffy; fold in whipped cream. Divide and spread evenly into pie crusts; chill until firm. Makes 16 servings.

Instead of cutting the stem out of pumpkins to be carved, cut the hole at the bottom. It'll sit evenly over a candle for a festive welcome from the porch.

desserts

Berry Crumble

Sandy Bernards
Valencia, CA

Try it with cherries too!

4 c. blackberries or blueberries
1 to 2 T. sugar
3 T. butter, softened

3 1-1/2 oz. pkgs. instant
oatmeal with maple and
brown sugar

Toss berries and sugar together in an ungreased 9" pie pan; set aside.
Cut butter into oatmeal until coarse crumbs form; sprinkle over berries.
Bake at 375 degrees until topping is golden, about 30 to 35 minutes.
Serves 6.

Dress up a shiny galvanized pail with a coat of orange paint and a
smiling Jack-O-Lantern face. It'll be perfect for keeping
drinks cool at the bonfire and so festive for
holding tricks & treats!

Pecan Bites

Hope Davenport
Portland, TX

So sweet, there's no need for frosting.

1 c. brown sugar, packed
1/2 c. all-purpose flour
1 c. chopped pecans

2/3 c. butter, melted
2 eggs, beaten

Combine sugar, flour and pecans; set aside. Blend butter and eggs together; mix into flour mixture. Fill greased and floured mini muffin tins 2/3 full; bake at 350 degrees for 22 to 25 minutes. Cool on a wire rack. Makes about 1-1/2 dozen.

Fill a shiny colander with plump red apples and mini pumpkins for an easy harvest centerpiece...tie on a gingham ribbon and tuck in a few sprigs of bittersweet too!

desserts

Autumn Apple Crisp

Joy Duncan
Kane, PA

Serve with a scoop of cinnamon or vanilla ice cream.

8 to 10 apples, cored, peeled
    and sliced
3/4 c. brown sugar, packed

3/4 c. biscuit baking mix
1/4 c. butter, melted
1 T. cinnamon

Layer apples in the bottom of a lightly buttered 13"x9" casserole dish; set aside. Combine sugar, baking mix, butter and cinnamon; crumble over apples. Bake at 350 degrees for 25 to 30 minutes; cool for 5 minutes. Makes 10 servings.

Cinnamon Poached Pears

Melanie Lowe
Dover, DE

A light dessert that's not too sweet, or serve as
a delicious side dish for roast chicken.

4 pears
1 c. pear nectar
1 c. water
3/4 c. maple syrup

2 4-inch cinnamon sticks,
    slightly crushed
4 strips lemon zest

Peel and core pears from the bottom, leaving stems intact. Cut a thin slice off bottom so pears will stand up; set aside. Combine remaining ingredients in a saucepan. Bring to a boil over medium heat, stirring occasionally. Add pears, standing right-side up. Reduce heat and simmer, covered, for 20 to 30 minutes, until tender. Remove pears from pan. Continue to simmer sauce in pan until reduced to 3/4 cup, about 15 minutes. Serve pears drizzled with sauce. Serves 4.

Sew a few old-fashioned yo-yo's out of orange fabric scraps and secure the middle with a button. Add a little green square for the stem and string together for a fun harvest garland!

autumn

Cookies & Cream Dessert

Linda Smolinske
Avilla, IN

The taste of our favorite cookie in a creamy dessert.

20-oz. pkg. chocolate sandwich
  cookies, crushed
1/4 c. margarine, melted
2 8-oz. pkgs. cream cheese,
  softened

2 8-oz. containers frozen
  whipped topping, thawed
  and divided
2 4-oz. pkgs. instant chocolate
  pudding mix

Mix cookie crumbs with margarine; press into the bottom of an
ungreased 13"x9" baking pan. Combine cream cheese with one
container of whipped topping; spread over cookie crust. Prepare
pudding according to package directions; layer on top of cream cheese
mixture. Top with remaining whipped topping; refrigerate until firm.
Makes 15 servings.

Search the farmers' markets and the pumpkin patch for
moonglow pumpkins and light yellow gourds. Their muted colors
look so pretty against bright red and gold autumn leaves.

desserts

Quick Chocolate Cookies

*Roberta Scheeler
Ashley, OH*

The easiest cookies ever!

9-oz. pkg. devil's food cake mix
1 egg

1 T. shortening, melted
1/2 c. chopped nuts

Blend ingredients and 2 tablespoons water together; drop by teaspoonfuls onto ungreased baking sheets. Bake at 350 degrees for 10 minutes. Makes 2 dozen.

Butter Cookies

*Jutta Hollingsworth
Denham Springs, LA*

Since you use a cookie press, these are so easy to fix anytime!

1 c. butter
2/3 c. sugar
3 egg yolks

1 t. vanilla extract
2-1/2 c. all-purpose flour

Combine butter, sugar, egg yolks and vanilla together; add flour, mixing by hand. Spoon mixture into a cookie press; press onto an ungreased baking sheet using desired discs. Bake at 400 degrees for 7 to 10 minutes. Makes 4 dozen.

Caramel Fudge Cake

Victoria Alzza
South Amboy, NJ

Try it with a buttery yellow cake mix too!

18-1/4 oz. pkg. chocolate
  cake mix
1/2 c. margarine
14-oz. pkg. caramels,
  unwrapped

14-oz. can sweetened condensed
  milk
1 c. chopped pecans

Prepare cake according to package directions; pour 2 cups of batter into a greased 13"x9" baking pan. Bake at 350 degrees for 15 minutes; set aside. In a saucepan, melt margarine and caramels; remove from heat. Add milk; stir well. Pour over cake; spread remaining cake batter over caramel mixture. Sprinkle with pecans; bake for an additional 30 minutes. Cool before serving. Makes 15 servings.

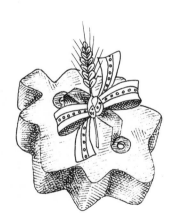

Transfer gilded imprints of fall foliage onto simple cotton napkins in no time. Using a foam brush, apply a little gold paint to the backs of collected oak, maple or sycamore leaves and stamp away...just right for Thanksgiving dinner!

Winter

In Winter, when the fields are white,
I sing this song for your delight.
- Lewis Carroll

Winter

Mixed-Up Meatball Dip

Julie Trumble
Battle Creek, MI

Makes enough for the whole party!

1 lb. ground beef, browned
1 lb. ground sausage, browned
2 16-oz. pkgs. pasteurized
    process hot Mexican cheese
    spread, cubed

4 10-3/4 oz. cans cream of
    mushroom soup

Combine beef and sausage in a heavy skillet; add cheese. Heat
until cheese is melted; mix in soup, stirring until warmed through.
Serves 24.

Quick Meatballs

Carolyn Magyar
Ebensburg, PA

Make 'em ahead...they freeze well.

2 lbs. ground beef
1/4 lb. ground sausage

6-oz. pkg. beef-flavored stuffing
    mix
3 eggs, beaten

Mix all ingredients together; shape into one-inch balls. Arrange on an
ungreased baking sheet; bake at 350 degrees for 30 to 45 minutes.
Makes about 4 dozen.

Look for die-cut wood shapes at craft stores...pick up an apple, a pig
or even an old-fashioned milk bottle. Paint with 2 coats of
chalkboard paint and add a stick-on magnet to the back.
Hang on the fridge for a quick & easy memo board.

appetizers

Sauerkraut Balls

Madge Bowman
Shreve, OH

The secret? Mix ingredients by hand and they'll hold their shape.

1 lb. ground sausage
14-oz. can sauerkraut, drained
1-3/4 to 3 c. long-cooking oats,
    uncooked

2 eggs, beaten

Mix ingredients together; roll into one-inch balls. Arrange on an ungreased baking sheet; bake at 325 degrees until done, about 20 minutes. Makes 40 servings.

Spruce up child-size chairs and add charm to a favorite nook. Add a new coat of paint and a couple of sparkling old-fashioned glass finials. Just drill 2 holes in the chair rails and the finials screw right in!

Stuffing & Seafood Bites

Marcia Marcoux
Charlton, MA

Great appetizers for all those holiday open houses!

1-1/2 c. herb-flavored stuffing
   mix
8-oz. can minced clams with
   juice

1 t. lemon juice
1/2 lb. bacon, slices halved

Combine first 3 ingredients together; shape one teaspoonful mixture
into a ball. Wrap one slice bacon around each ball; secure with a
toothpick. Place on an ungreased baking sheet; repeat with remaining
mixture. Bake at 350 degrees until bacon is crisp, about 20 to
25 minutes. Makes about 2 dozen.

A new twist on the gift of a favorite recipe! Give a copy of the
cookbook it's in and the ingredients to make the special dish...
bundle it all up in a pretty basket or new mixing bowl.

appetizers

Shrimp Dip

Becky Newton
Oklahoma City, OK

Serve with crispy bread sticks or bagel chips.

2 8-oz. pkgs. cream cheese,
   softened
4-1/2 oz. can shrimp, drained

1/4 c. butter
2 green onions, chopped

Mix all ingredients together; cover and refrigerate until serving. Makes about 2-1/2 cups.

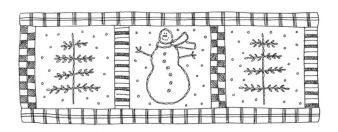

Cheesy Crab Spread

Shari Yanagi
Honolulu, HI

So quick & easy to make in the microwave.

1 c. shredded Cheddar cheese
1 c. shredded mozzarella cheese
3 cloves garlic, minced

1/2 c. imitation crabmeat,
   shredded
1 c. mayonnaise

Combine ingredients together in a microwave-safe serving bowl; mix well. Microwave on high setting in 30 second intervals, stirring well until cheese melts and mixture is warmed. Makes about 3 cups.

Bacon-Cheese Puffs

*Irene Robinson
Cincinnati, OH*

Easy and delicious, these disappear quickly!

1 lb. bacon, crisply cooked and
   crumbled
2-1/2 c. shredded Cheddar
   cheese

2 T. mustard
1 c. mayonnaise
1 loaf sliced party pumpernickel

Combine bacon, cheese, mustard and mayonnaise together; spoon
onto each slice of bread. Arrange on an ungreased baking sheet; broil
until bubbly, about 5 minutes. Makes 30 servings.

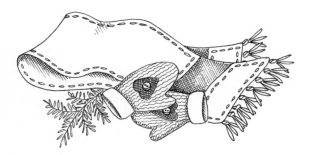

Jalapeño-Cheese Squares

*Holly Moore
Lufkin, TX*

So easy and SO good.

12 eggs, beaten
1 lb. Cheddar cheese, cubed

chopped jalapeños to taste

Mix ingredients together; spread in a lightly buttered 13"x9" baking
pan. Bake at 350 degrees for 30 minutes; cool and cut into squares
to serve. Makes 15 to 18 servings.

Party Cheese Ball

Jennifer Eveland-Kupp
Reading, PA

You'll be asked to make this recipe over and over again.

8-oz. pkg. pasteurized process
    cheese spread
3-oz. pkg. deviled ham spread

8-oz. pkg. cream cheese,
    softened
1 c. chopped nuts

Mix first 3 ingredients together; form into a ball. Roll in nuts; wrap in plastic wrap and refrigerate until serving. Serves 8.

Look for decorative 5-inch tiles at the hardware store...glue a 5-inch square of cork to the back. Line up your favorite designs along the back of the counter and they'll be ready to act as trivets under hot pots and plates!

Spicy Buffalo Chicken Wings

Rosalyn Odion
Yorba Linda, CA

Serve with celery and blue cheese dressing.

2-1/2 lbs. chicken wings
4-oz. bottle hot pepper sauce

1/2 c. butter, melted
2 T. white vinegar

Arrange chicken in a 13"x9" greased baking pan; bake at 425 degrees for one hour, turning frequently. Remove from oven; set aside. Whisk hot sauce, butter and vinegar together; pour over chicken. Toss gently to coat. Serves 4 to 6.

Take advantage of the finished edges of vintage-style dish towels and transform them into pretty pillows in minutes! Using a straight stitch, leave a margin of about 2 inches on 3 sides, stuff and finish stitching across the fourth side. Add buttons, ribbon or trim along the edges, if desired.

appetizers

Sausage-Cheese Spread

Pam South
Villa Hills, KY

Spread on rye rounds and bake until warmed.

1 lb. ground beef
1 lb. ground sausage
16-oz. pkg. pasteurized process
   cheese spread, cubed

1/2 t. dried oregano
1/2 t. garlic powder

Brown ground beef and sausage together; drain. Reduce heat; add remaining ingredients, stirring until cheese melts. Makes about 4 cups.

Snuggle Up

Garlic-Artichoke Dip

Valeri Audino
Olmsted Falls, OH

Serve with toasted pita triangles…yum!

1 c. mayonnaise
1 c. grated Parmesan cheese
14-oz. can artichoke hearts,
   chopped

2 cloves garlic, minced
14-oz. pkg. frozen chopped
   spinach, cooked and drained

Combine ingredients together; mix well. Spread in an ungreased 9" pie pan; bake at 250 degrees for 30 minutes. Makes about 4-1/2 cups.

Winter

Bacon-Stuffed Mushrooms

Robyn Wright
Delaware, OH

Rich and cheesy, these won't last long!

2 lbs. whole mushrooms, stems
   removed and reserved
1/2 onion, minced
8 slices bacon, crisply cooked
   and crumbled, drippings
   reserved

12-oz. pkg. cream cheese,
   softened
1 c. shredded Cheddar cheese

Chop stems of mushrooms; mix in onion. Sauté until tender; stir in bacon. Reduce heat; stir in cream cheese until melted. Remove from heat; spoon cheese mixture into mushroom caps. Arrange side-by-side on a greased baking sheet; sprinkle with Cheddar cheese. Bake at 350 degrees for 15 minutes. Makes 10 to 12 servings.

Frame a photo for a loved one and decorate a simple frame with candy conversation hearts...how sweet! Brush some clear sealant over the hearts to keep them looking bright.

appetizers

Wrapped Water Chestnuts

Jan Fishback
Carmi, IL

Crunchy with just the right amount of sweetness.

1 lb. bacon, slices halved
16-oz. can whole water
   chestnuts

1/2 c. mayonnaise
1/2 c. brown sugar, packed
1/4 c. chili sauce

Cook bacon until almost crisp; drain. Wrap one slice around each water chestnut; secure with a toothpick. Arrange in an ungreased 9"x9" baking pan; set aside. Mix remaining ingredients together; pour over water chestnuts. Bake at 350 degrees for 45 minutes. Makes about 2 dozen.

Brie Kisses

Kathy Grashoff
Fort Wayne, IN

Little cheesy bites...perfect for holiday parties!

2/3 lb. Brie cheese
17.3-oz. pkg. frozen puff pastry

hot pepper jelly

Cut Brie into 1/2-inch cubes; arrange on a plate and place in the freezer. Let pastry thaw at room temperature for 30 minutes; unfold each pastry and roll with a rolling pin to remove creases. Slice each sheet into quarters; slice each quarter in half. Cut each piece in half one more time for a total of 32 squares. Place one square into a greased mini muffin cup; arrange so corners of dough point upwards. Repeat with remaining dough. Put one Brie cube in center of each cup; top each with 1/4 teaspoon hot pepper jelly. Bake at 400 degrees for 10 to 15 minutes. Makes 32.

After the festivities are over, hang the popcorn garland outside for the birds...a holiday treat for our feathered friends.

Garlic-Cheese Biscuits

Corinne Cloward
Eagle Mountain, UT

Melt-in-your-mouth goodness.

2 c. biscuit baking mix
1/2 t. garlic powder
1 c. shredded Cheddar cheese

2/3 c. milk
2 T. butter, melted

Combine biscuit mix, garlic powder and cheese; make a well in the center. Add milk; stir until well mixed. Drop by tablespoonfuls onto a greased baking sheet; bake at 450 degrees for 10 to 12 minutes. Brush with butter and serve while warm. Makes 8 to 10.

One kind word can warm three winter months.
- Japanese Proverb

soups & breads

Easy Potato Soup

Jeanne West
Roanoke Rapids, NC

Served piping hot, there's nothing better.

4 to 5 potatoes, peeled and
  cubed
10-3/4 oz. can cream of
  celery soup
10-3/4 oz. can cream of
  chicken soup

1-1/4 c. milk
7.6-oz. pkg. instant mashed
  potato flakes

Place potatoes, soups and one soup can water in a slow cooker; heat on high setting until potatoes are tender, about 2 to 3 hours. Add milk and enough instant mashed potatoes to reach desired consistency, stirring constantly. Heat 2 to 3 hours longer; spoon into bowls to serve. Serves 4 to 6.

Use flea market finds to make one-of-a-kind picture hangers. Small drawer knobs or old-fashioned clothes hooks can be used...just add a screw and hang the picture from a wide ribbon.

Mini Dinner Rolls

Carol Thomson
Abilene, TX

This batter keeps in the refrigerator for up to 7 days when stored in an airtight container...just make 'em as needed.

1 pkg. active dry yeast
3/4 c. oil

4 c. self-rising flour
1/4 c. sugar

Dissolve yeast in 2 cups warm water; set aside until foamy, 5 to 10 minutes. Add remaining ingredients; mix well. Fill greased or paper-lined mini muffin tins 3/4 full; bake at 400 degrees for 15 minutes. Makes 3 to 4 dozen.

Clippings of holly, boxwood or evergreen will welcome Winter when placed inside a nostalgic tin coffee pot. Stamp on some stars or paint a whimsical checkerboard, if desired.

soups & breads

Slow-Cooker Smoked Sausage Stew

Susie Gray
Winchester, IN

Bake a pan of cornbread to serve alongside.

4 to 5 potatoes, peeled and
  cubed
2 16-oz. cans green beans,
  undrained

1-lb. pkg. smoked sausage,
  sliced
1 onion, chopped
2 T. butter

Layer potatoes, green beans, sausage and onion in a slow cooker; dot with butter. Heat on low setting for 4 to 5 hours. Makes 4 servings.

Missouri Hobo Stew

Billie Brazeal
Carlin, NV

Everyone from college kids to our friend from Australia loves this dish!

1-1/2 lbs. ground beef
1 onion, chopped
3 10-3/4 oz. cans minestrone
  soup

2 15-oz. cans ranch-style beans
10-oz. can tomatoes with chiles

Brown ground beef and onion together; drain. Combine all ingredients in a slow cooker; heat on low setting for 8 to 10 hours, stirring occasionally. Makes 6 to 8 servings.

Indian Fry Bread

Amber Brandt
Tucson, AZ

*We eat them plain, sprinkled with powdered sugar or
drizzled with honey.*

2 c. all-purpose flour
1-1/2 t. baking powder
1/2 t. salt

1 T. powdered milk
oil for deep frying

Combine first 4 ingredients; pour 3/4 cup warm water on top. Use
hands to combine; knead on a lightly floured surface until dough is
smooth and elastic. Divide dough into 1-1/2 inch rounds; roll each
out into a flattened circle. Heat 1/4-inch depth oil to 365 degrees in a
10" skillet; add dough, heating until golden. Turn to heat other side;
drain on paper towels. Serves 6 to 8.

Wired ribbon in festive holiday patterns and prints dress up
terra cotta pots on the patio and porch.

soups & breads

Chicken & Dumplin' Soup

Brenda Hancock
Hartford, KY

Comfort food at its finest.

10-3/4 oz. can cream of
    chicken soup
4 c. chicken broth
4 boneless, skinless chicken
    breasts, cooked and
    shredded

2 15-oz. cans mixed vegetables
2 12-oz. tubes refrigerated
    biscuits, quartered

Bring soup and broth to a slow boil in a saucepan over medium heat;
whisk until smooth. Stir in chicken and vegetables; bring to a boil.
Drop biscuit quarters into soup; cover and simmer for 15 minutes. Let
soup sit for 10 minutes before serving. Serves 4 to 6.

Corned Beef & Cabbage Stew

Faye Newton
Connersville, IN

Grandma Nutty was famous for this stew...whenever company
would show up unexpectedly, she'd just add a can of corn or
green beansso there'd be enough for everyone!

5 potatoes, peeled and chopped
5 carrots, peeled and chopped
28-oz. can crushed tomatoes

1 head cabbage, shredded
12-oz. pkg. corned beef,
    chopped

Add potatoes, carrots and tomatoes to a stockpot; heat until vegetables
are tender, about 20 minutes. Reduce heat; stir in cabbage and corned
beef. Simmer for 20 minutes. Serves 4.

Winter

Saucy Pizza Casserole

Pat Mollohan
Parkersburg, WV

*Make it a supreme with any other favorite pizza
toppings...olives, mushrooms or peppers!*

16-oz. pkg. elbow macaroni,
    cooked
3 14-oz. jars pizza sauce
8-oz. pkg. sliced pepperoni

8-oz. pkg. diced pepperoni
8 to 10-oz. pkg. shredded
    mozzarella cheese

Combine ingredients together; mix gently. Spread into an ungreased
2-quart casserole or 13"x9" baking pan; bake at 350 degrees for 35 to
45 minutes. Serves 6.

Giving a tin of homemade goodies for Christmas this year? Make it
easier for little hands to open them up by gluing a pretty ribbon
inside the lid. Leave a loop of ribbon hanging out of the tin
and they can just pull up on it to get to the goodies!

soups & breads

Chicken Chili with Green Salsa

Kathy Grashoff
Fort Wayne, IN

Spicy and warm, this is sure to chase the chill away!

12-oz. pkg. chicken breast
    tenders, cut into 1/2-inch
    strips
2 15-1/2 oz. cans white kidney
    beans, rinsed and drained

16-oz. jar mild green salsa
1/4 c. fresh cilantro, chopped
Optional: cherry tomatoes

Place chicken in a skillet; sauté for 2 to 3 minutes or until juices run clear when chicken is pierced with a fork. Add beans, salsa, cilantro and 1/2 cup water; heat thoroughly, about 5 minutes. Spoon into serving bowls; top with quartered tomatoes, if desired. Serves 4.

Quick & Easy Chili

Carol Shirkey
Canton, OH

This recipe was given to me many years ago by a close friend. Since then, it's become a dinnertime regular at our house.
Just as yummy, if not better, the next day!

2 lbs. ground beef
2 T. oil
2 15-oz. cans kidney beans,
    drained and rinsed

2 10-3/4 oz. cans tomato soup
2 T. chili powder

Brown ground beef in oil; drain. Add remaining ingredients and one soup can water; stir well. Bring to a boil; reduce heat, cover and simmer for one hour. Makes 6 to 8 servings.

Winter

Homestyle Spoon Bread

Tonia Holm
Burlington, ND

*My mother grew up with this bread during the Depression. It looks
like an English muffin but the inside is very soft...wonderful
with butter and a cup of tea!*

1 c. all-purpose flour
2 t. baking powder
1 t. sugar

1/2 t. salt
oil for deep frying

Mix ingredients together; blend in 3/4 cup water. Drop by
tablespoonfuls into a heavy skillet filled with 1/4-inch depth hot oil.
Flip over when bubbles form along the edges; heat until golden
on each side. Serves 4.

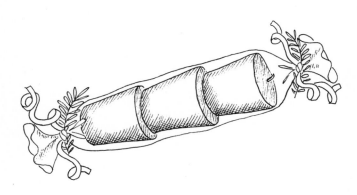

Lay votives end-to-end and roll up in tulle...tie the ends with curly
ribbon for a festive stocking stuffer or package tie-on!

Hearty Beef Stew

Nadine Thomas
Valley Forge, PA

Serve with warm rolls and a salad.

10-1/2 oz. can French onion
   soup
10-3/4 oz. can tomato soup
1 lb. stew beef

5 to 6 redskin potatoes,
   quartered
8-oz. can baby carrots

Combine ingredients together; pour into an ungreased 13"x9" baking pan. Cover with aluminum foil; bake at 350 degrees for 1-1/2 to 2 hours. Serves 4 to 5.

Combine one cup cinnamon and 3/4 cup applesauce with 2 tablespoons craft glue to make cinnamon-apple ornaments. Roll out dough, cut with cookie cutters and let dry...hang on a tree or in the center of a wreath!

Winter

Winter Salad

Kimberly Hornberger Allabaugh
Middleburg, PA

A simple salad that will remind you of deviled eggs.

1 head lettuce, torn
1 c. sugar
1 c. mayonnaise

2 T. mustard
4 eggs, hard-boiled and peeled

Place lettuce in a large serving bowl; set aside. Whisk sugar, mayonnaise and mustard together; pour over lettuce. Slice hard-boiled eggs; add to lettuce mixture. Toss gently before serving. Serves 6.

Take a walk out in the snow and hunt for pine cones...the whole family can go. Stack them in a basket or tie on ribbons to make ornaments to share!

Salads & Sides

Cabbage-Rice Casserole

Jean Gallant
New Bedford, MA

Tastes just like traditional cabbage rolls without all the work!

1 head cabbage, shredded
1 c. long-cooking rice, uncooked

2 lbs. ground beef, browned
28-oz. jar spaghetti sauce

Place cabbage in the bottom of a greased 13"x9" baking pan; spread rice on top. Pour 2 cups water over rice; spoon beef over top. Pour sauce evenly over beef; bake, uncovered, at 375 degrees for 1-1/2 to 2 hours. Mix together before serving. Serves 6.

Super Potato Casserole

Wendy Lee Paffenroth
Pine Island, NY

My sister gave me this recipe...her 6-year-old son loves it!
Great alongside homemade meat loaf.

1/4 c. oil
5 potatoes, sliced
1/2 c. milk

1 c. shredded Cheddar cheese
1 c. corn flake cereal, crushed
Garnish: garlic powder

Place oil in a plastic bag; drop potato slices in bag, shaking to coat. Arrange potatoes in an ungreased 13"x9" glass baking dish; pour milk on top. In a separate bowl, mix cheese and cereal together; spread over potatoes. Cover; bake at 350 degrees for 30 to 45 minutes. Uncover and bake for 5 to 10 more minutes. Serves 6.

Force tulip or crocus bulbs in a planter surrounded by colored glass marbles or smooth rocks...keep them watered and their blooms will add color to a winter mantel.

Winter

Savory Limas

Marilou Dolan
Great Falls, VA

This delicious and unusual side dish will get requests for the recipe.

10-oz. pkg. frozen baby lima
    beans
3 cloves garlic, chopped

1 T. butter
whipping cream
nutmeg to taste

Boil lima beans and garlic in water until soft, about 12 to 18 minutes; drain. Stir in butter; blend with an electric blender, adding just enough cream to reach mashed potato consistency. Sprinkle with nutmeg to taste. Serves 4.

Place a bundle of bare branches in a sand-filled galvanized bucket and set it out on the front porch. Weave little white fairy lights throughout the branches for a magical sparkle.

Salads & Sides

Garlic-Butter Orzo

*Gail Prather
Bethel, MN*

Add shredded chicken for a meal in itself!

1 c. orzo, cooked
2 T. butter
2 cloves garlic, chopped

1 T. lemon juice
2 T. fresh parsley, chopped

Place orzo in a serving bowl and set aside. Melt butter in a 12" skillet over medium-high heat; sauté garlic until golden. Remove from heat; add lemon juice, stirring well. Pour over orzo; add parsley and toss. Makes 4 to 6 servings.

French-Fried Cauliflower

*Roseann Haley
Cutler, IN*

Kids love it and will remember it forever!

1 head cauliflower, cut into
   flowerets
3 eggs, beaten

1 sleeve round buttery crackers,
   crushed
oil for deep frying

Dip cauliflower into eggs; coat with cracker crumbs. Deep fry in a heavy skillet with 1/2-inch depth oil until golden; drain on paper towels. Makes 6 to 8 servings.

Stringing popcorn and cranberries for the tree? Tie on some tin cookie cutters too!

Winter

Cranberry-Spinach Salad

Lori Wallace
Covina, CA

Sweet, colorful and oh-so tasty!

2 bunches spinach leaves, torn
1/4 c. feta cheese, crumbled
1/4 c. sweetened, dried
   cranberries

3/4 c. raspberry vinaigrette
   salad dressing
1/4 c. slivered almonds

Combine ingredients in a large serving bowl; toss gently. Makes 6 to 8 servings.

Deliver a dose of sunshine to a dear friend on a snowy afternoon.
Fill a galvanized pail with oranges, tie on a bow and leave
it on their doorstep...how sweet!

Salads & Sides

Baked Potato Salad

Kathie Williams
Oakland City, IN

Double the recipe for family gatherings...I use a large disposable aluminum pan for quick clean-up!

13 to 15 potatoes, cooked and cubed
1-1/2 to 2 lbs. bacon, crisply cooked and crumbled
3 c. shredded Cheddar cheese, divided

1 onion, chopped
16-oz. jar mayonnaise-type salad dressing

Combine potatoes, bacon, half the cheese, onion and enough salad dressing to make the mixture moist; mix well. Spread into a large roasting pan; sprinkle with remaining cheese. Bake at 350 degrees until bubbly, about one hour. Serves 18 to 20.

Wilted Lettuce Salad

Amy Steiner
Illiopolis, IL

Just the 2 of you for dinner? Halve the recipe and make just enough.

10 c. salad greens, torn
1/2 c. green onions, sliced
1/2 c. vinegar

2 T. sugar
1/4 lb. bacon, crisply cooked and crumbed, drippings reserved

Combine salad greens and green onions in a large serving bowl; set aside. Whisk vinegar, sugar and 1/4 cup water together until sugar dissolves; set aside. Heat 2 tablespoons reserved bacon drippings to boiling; slowly whisk in vinegar mixture. Bring to a boil; remove from heat. Pour over salad; top with bacon. Toss and serve immediately. Makes 4 to 6 servings.

Newlywed Beef & Noodles

Shannon Kennedy
Delaware, OH

I was just recently married and this is one of my first original recipes.

1 lb. stew beef, browned
3 14-1/2 oz. cans beef broth

3 to 4 cubes beef bouillon
8-oz. pkg. egg noodles

Add beef, broth and 3 broth cans water to a slow cooker; stir in bouillon cubes. Heat on low to medium setting for 4 to 6 hours; add noodles. Heat on low setting until noodles are done. Serves 4.

Surprise newlyweds with dressed-up towels...sew washable ribbon onto plain bath and hand towels in coordinating colors.
For a no-sew version, use iron-on adhesive
to secure ribbon in place!

mains

Mom's Meat Loaf

Susan Biffignani
Fenton, MO

I make this often for friends feeling under the weather...
it's always a hit.

2 to 3 lbs. ground beef
1 egg
10 to 12 saltine crackers,
   crushed

3/4 c. catsup, divided
1/4 c. onion, diced

Combine ground beef, egg, crackers, 1/4 cup catsup and onion
together; pat into an ungreased 9"x5" loaf pan. Spread remaining
catsup on top; bake at 350 degrees for one hour or until center is no
longer pink. Makes 8 servings.

Easy Veggie Bake

Margie Schaffner
Altoona, IA

A recipe we tried at the lake last summer...we all loved it!

16-oz. pkg. frozen broccoli,
   carrots and cauliflower
10-3/4 oz. can cream of
   mushroom soup

8-oz. pkg. vegetable-flavored
   cream cheese, softened
1/2 to 1 c. seasoned croutons

Prepare vegetables according to package directions; drain and place in
a large mixing bowl. Stir in soup and cream cheese; mix well. Spread
into a greased one-quart casserole dish; sprinkle with croutons. Bake,
uncovered, at 375 degrees until bubbly, about 25 minutes. Makes
4 to 6 servings.

Winter

Scalloped Potatoes & Ham

Julie Derks
Appleton, WI

Fix it in the morning and come home to a hearty dinner.

2 to 3 lbs. potatoes, peeled,
  sliced and divided
3/4-lb. pkg. cooked ham, cubed
  and divided
1 onion, sliced and divided

2 c. shredded Cheddar cheese,
  divided
10-3/4 oz. can cream of
  celery soup

Layer a third each of the potatoes, ham, onion and cheese in a
well-greased slow cooker; repeat 2 times. Spread soup on top; heat
on low setting for 7 to 8 hours. Stir occasionally. Serves 4.

Make a memo board in the blink of an eye! Cover a piece of
plywood with cotton batting and fabric stapled into place on the
back. Create a latticework of ribbon overtop, pull taut and secure
with straight pins around the edges...staple in place on the back. Slip
vintage photos, postcards or other mementos behind the ribbon!

mains

Mary's Pork Chops

Mary Brennan
Hollywood, FL

My family loves these tender pork chops with mashed potatoes...the gravy is really delicious.

1 egg
1-1/2 c. milk
6 boneless pork chops

2 c. bread crumbs
14-1/2 oz. can beef broth

Beat egg and milk together; set aside. Dip pork chops in egg mixture; coat with bread crumbs. Brown on both sides in a 12" skillet, adding a bit of oil, if necessary. Pour broth over the pork chops; simmer until fork tender, about one hour. Makes 6 servings.

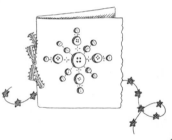

Pork Chops & Rice

Caroline Trinidad
McAlester, OK

Try adding a fresh sliced jalapeño before baking for added zest.

4 to 8 pork chops
1-1/2 oz. pkg. onion soup mix

2 green peppers, sliced and
  divided
1 c. long-cooking rice, uncooked

Sauté pork chops in a 12" skillet until browned on both sides; remove to a platter. Add soup mix and 2 cups water to same skillet; stir and heat until mix dissolves. Layer half the green peppers in an ungreased 13"x9" baking pan; sprinkle with rice. Arrange pork chops on top; pour soup mixture over the pork chops. Top with remaining peppers; cover and bake at 325 degrees for 45 minutes to one hour. Serves 4 to 8.

Pot Roast Casserole

Sandy Rowe
Bellevue, OH

So easy and your family will gobble it right up.

8-oz. pkg. fine egg noodles,
   cooked
2 c. pot roast, cooked and
   chopped

2 c. Alfredo sauce
1 c. sliced mushrooms
1/4 c. bread crumbs

Mix noodles, pot roast, Alfredo sauce and mushrooms in an ungreased
2-quart casserole dish; sprinkle with bread crumbs. Bake
at 350 degrees for 20 to 30 minutes or until crumbs are golden.
Serves 4.

Roasted Rosemary Beef

Sue Garver
Riley, KS

There's no other liquid necessary for this make-ahead dish.

3 to 4-lb. pot roast
3 cubes beef bouillon, crushed
1 T. fresh rosemary, chopped

1/2 t. garlic powder
seasoning salt and pepper to
   taste

Place roast into slow cooker that has been coated with non-stick
vegetable spray. Add bouillon cubes and seasonings. Turn slow cooker
on low; heat for 8 to 10 hours. Makes 6 to 8 servings.

Make your own homespun ribbon
for wrapping up country gifts! Just
tear vintage-style fabric along the grain.
For a truly vintage look, try tea-staining
the fabric. What could be easier?

mains

Yummy Meat Pie

Marcella Meese
Wilmot, OH

*We enjoy several of these pies at our family brunch
on Christmas morning!*

8-oz. tube refrigerated crescent
   rolls, separated and divided
10-oz. pkg. Swiss cheese, cubed

1-lb. pkg. smoked sausage,
   sliced
2 eggs, beaten
8 to 10 slices pepperoni, diced

Line a 9" greased pie pan with 5 crescent rolls; lightly press seams
together. Mix remaining ingredients; spread in crust. Roll remaining
3 rolls thinly; cut into strips. Crisscross over top of pie. Bake at
325 degrees for 50 to 60 minutes. Let sit 10 minutes before slicing.
Makes 8 servings.

Sparkling hard-tack candy looks so pretty surrounding a
candle in an old-fashioned candy dish.

Lazy Man's Cabbage Rolls

Ernestine Dobson
Parsons, KS

Fast and easy to fix!

1 lb. ground beef, browned
1 onion, diced
3 T. instant rice, uncooked

16-oz. can diced tomatoes
4 c. cabbage, chopped

Simmer first 4 ingredients in a saucepan for 5 minutes; drain. Spread cabbage in an ungreased 13"x9" baking pan; pour ground beef mixture on top. Cover and bake at 350 degrees for one hour; do not stir. Serves 6.

Use old dresser drawers for everything from under-bed storage bins to whimsical window boxes outside. Spruce up small drawers with a new coat of paint and some fun hardware...fill with cookbooks in the kitchen too!

Vegetable Meat Loaf

Lynn Williams
Muncie, IN

*Pour tomato sauce over the top during the last 1/2 hour of baking
for an extra-juicy topping.*

1-1/2 lbs. ground beef
1.4-oz. pkg. vegetable soup mix
1 egg, beaten

1/2 c. bread crumbs
1/3 to 1/2 c. milk

Combine ingredients in a mixing bowl; mix well. Shape into an
8"x4" loaf; place on an aluminum foil-lined baking sheet. Bake at
350 degrees for one hour. Let stand 10 minutes before slicing. Makes
4 to 6 servings.

Oven Beef & Noodles

Kristie Rigo
Friedens, PA

A hearty stick-to-your-ribs dish we all crave on cold winter days.

1-1/2 oz. pkg. onion soup mix
4 c. water
10-3/4 oz. can cream of
    mushroom soup

3-lb. boneless beef chuck roast
12-oz. pkg. kluski egg noodles,
    uncooked

Combine soup mix and water in a roasting pan; stir in soup. Place
roast in pan on top of soup mixture. Cover and bake at 350 degrees
for 4 hours, or until meat is very tender. Remove roast from pan and
shred; return to pan. Add noodles to pan; reduce heat to 300 degrees.
Cover and bake for 20 to 30 minutes, stirring every 15 minutes until
noodles are tender. Add water if necessary to prevent drying out.
Makes 6 to 8 servings.

Toss some plump pine cones with a few drops of cinnamon oil and
just a little glitter in a plastic zipping bag. Give it a shake and
set them all along the mantel...so easy and sparkly!

Winter

Easy Tamale Casserole

Jan Durston
Norco, CA

Frozen tamales make this recipe a snap!

12 frozen tamales, partially
    thawed
2 14-3/4 oz. cans creamed corn

8-oz. can chiles
2 c. shredded Cheddar cheese

Slice tamales in half lengthwise; arrange half with the cut-side up in an ungreased 13"x9" baking pan. Spread one can creamed corn and chiles on top; layer on remaining tamale halves, cut-side down. Spread with remaining can creamed corn; bake at 350 degrees until bubbly, about 30 to 40 minutes. Sprinkle with cheese; return to oven until melted, about 5 to 8 minutes. Serves 6.

Transform terra cotta pots or bowls with hard candy...just glue wrapped candies all around the edges. Fill with treats and it'll be just right for giving homemade goodies at the holidays or anytime!

mains

Ricotta Fettuccine Sauce

Lorna Dressler
Universal City, TX

Rich and cheesy, we love it.

1 T. butter, melted
3/4 c. ricotta cheese
1/2 c. grated Parmesan cheese

1 tomato, chopped
2 T. fresh basil leaves, chopped

Combine ingredients together; spoon over hot fettuccine to serve.
Makes 4 servings.

Tomato-Feta Salad

Susan Dishong
Cumberland, MD

*Season with fresh herbs if you like...oregano, basil and chives are
easy to keep growing throughout the cold weather.*

2 pts. cherry tomatoes, halved
1 sweet onion, chopped
4-oz. pkg. feta cheese, crumbled

2/3 c. oil
1/3 c. red wine vinegar

Gently combine tomatoes, onion and cheese in a serving bowl; set
aside. Whisk oil and vinegar together; pour over tomato mixture. Toss
to coat; cover and refrigerate before serving. Serves 8 to 10.

Spruce up inexpensive baskets by trimming the edge with a
sparkly wired ribbon. Add a plastic liner and place 3 or 4 little
pots of herbs inside...an easy gift for any season!

Bacon-Wrapped Chicken

Brenda Burkett
Martinsburg, WV

Great tasting and easy to prepare, you can double the recipe for holiday company.

2 3-oz. pkgs. dried, chipped
  beef
8 boneless, skinless chicken
  breasts

16 slices bacon
10-3/4 oz. can cream of
  mushroom soup
1 c. sour cream

Line the bottom of an ungreased 13"x9" glass baking dish with chipped beef; set aside. Wrap each chicken breast with 2 slices of bacon; place on top of beef. Bake at 350 degrees for 30 minutes; spread soup and sour cream on top. Return to oven for an additional 40 minutes. Serves 6 to 8.

Looking for a way to dress up throw pillows? Trim them with big buttons, velvety trim or whimsical rick-rack for instant charm.

Chicken & Stuffing Casserole

Sandy Tolbert
Big Stone Gap, VA

This recipe can be made the day before...just store in the refrigerator until you're ready to bake and serve.

4 boneless, skinless chicken
   breasts, boiled and broth
   reserved
12-oz. pkg. stuffing mix
1/2 c. butter, melted

10-3/4 oz. can cream of
   mushroom soup
10-3/4 oz. can cream of
   chicken soup

Cool chicken; slice into cubes and set aside. Mix stuffing with butter; set aside. Whisk cream of mushroom soup and one soup can of reserved broth together; set aside. Repeat with cream of chicken soup; set aside. Layer a third of the stuffing mixture in a lightly buttered 2-quart casserole dish; continue layering with half the chicken, the mushroom soup mixture, another third of the stuffing, the remaining chicken, the cream of chicken soup mixture and then top with remaining stuffing. Bake in a 350-degree oven for 30 to 45 minutes. Makes 4 servings.

Lightly place paper doilies on a window and coat with spray snow... take away the doily for a dainty snowflake!

Ham & Potato Pie

Rachel Keller
Provo, UT

This is a favorite recipe my husband shared with me from his time living in Argentina.

2 9-inch pie crusts
3 potatoes, peeled and sliced
1/2 c. cooked ham, cubed

1/2 c. cheese, cubed
4 to 5 eggs, beaten

Arrange one pie crust in an ungreased 9" pie pan; set aside. Boil potatoes in water until tender; drain. Spread into pie crust; add ham and cheese. Pour eggs on top; cover with remaining crust. Pinch crusts together; vent top crust. Bake at 400 degrees for 45 to 50 minutes. Serves 8.

A new twist on gift bags...instead of folding the tops over, punch a hole in the top and close with a grosgrain ribbon. Attach beads or buttons to the ends of the ribbon, if desired.

Easy Chicken Pot Pie

Beth Jones
Tallassee, AL

Just right after a day of sledding!

2 9-inch deep-dish
   pie crusts
10-3/4 oz. can cream of
   chicken soup

15-oz. can mixed vegetables
5-oz. can chicken
2 T. butter, melted

Bring pie crusts to room temperature; set aside. Mix the next
3 ingredients together; set aside. Place one pie crust in an ungreased
9" deep-dish pie pan; pour vegetable mixture into pie crust. Roll out
remaining crust; arrange on top of pie. Seal and pinch edges; vent top
crust and brush with butter. Bake at 350 degrees until golden, about
30 to 40 minutes. Serves 8.

Kale & Potato Casserole

Jill Ross
Pickerington, OH

Warm potatoes, wilted greens and Parmesan cheese
make this a hearty side!

1/4 c. butter, melted
3 potatoes, thinly sliced
10 leaves kale, finely chopped

5 T. grated Parmesan cheese
salt and pepper to taste

In a bowl, drizzle butter over potatoes and mix well. Grease a cast-iron
skillet and arrange a layer of potatoes in the bottom. Top with 1/3 of
the kale, 1/3 of the cheese, salt and pepper. Continue layering, ending
with potatoes; sprinkle with remaining cheese. Cover with aluminum
foil and bake at 375 degrees for 30 minutes. Remove foil and bake for
another 15 to 30 minutes, until potatoes are tender. Serves 4 to 6.

Look for unfinished wood pieces at the craft store to make seasonal
decorating easy. Stencil or stamp tissue boxes, crates or picture
frames to welcome the holidays year 'round.

Poor Man's Cordon Bleu

Linda Lamb
Round Rock, TX

A quick & easy variation on a classic.

8-oz. pkg. cream cheese,
    softened
4 green onions, minced
garlic powder to taste

6 boneless, skinless chicken
    breasts
12 bacon strips

Combine cream cheese, onions and garlic powder together; set aside.
Flatten chicken breasts using a rolling pin; spread cream cheese
mixture down the center of each chicken breast; fold chicken in
half. Wrap 2 bacon strips around each chicken breast; secure with
toothpicks. Arrange in an ungreased 13"x9" baking pan; bake at
350 degrees for one hour. Makes 6 servings.

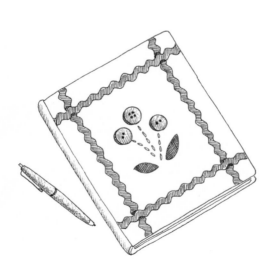

For a thoughtful gift, attach colorful ribbon or rick-rack along the
edges of a plain journal. Be sure to include a fun pen or pencil!

mains

Saucy Mozzarella Chicken

Theresa Beach
Lexington, SC

A real family pleaser, we serve it over angel hair pasta.

6 boneless, skinless chicken
   breasts
salt and pepper to taste

26-oz. jar spaghetti sauce
8-oz. pkg. shredded mozzarella
   cheese

Season chicken with salt and pepper; arrange in an ungreased 13"x9" baking pan. Pour spaghetti sauce on top; bake at 350 degrees for one hour and 10 minutes. Sprinkle with cheese; return to oven until melted, an additional 5 to 10 minutes. Serves 6.

Use red and white peppermints or other holiday hard candy to anchor a white taper candle inside a canning jar. Use mismatched jars for a charming look.

Peanut Butter Cups

La Verne Fang
Joliet, IL

Pop 'em in your mouth...betcha can't eat just one!

1/2 c. peanut butter
1/2 c. powdered sugar
1/2 c. powdered milk

4 T. corn syrup
12-oz. pkg. milk chocolate chips

Combine first 4 ingredients together in a mixing bowl; mix well. Set aside. Arrange 72 fluted paper candy cups on a baking sheet; set aside. Melt chocolate in a double boiler or microwave; spoon one teaspoon melted chocolate into one candy cup, tilting to cover the bottom. Add 1/4 teaspoon peanut butter mixture on top of chocolate; cover with one teaspoon melted chocolate. Repeat with remaining chocolate and peanut butter mixture; set aside to harden. Makes about 6 dozen.

Wow 'em with wallpaper! Make plain-jane frames extra special by covering them with wallpaper remnants...add ribbon or sparkly beads too.

desserts

Triple-Chocolate Fudge Bars

Jennifer Eveland-Kupp
Reading, PA

A hit with chocolate lovers everywhere.

4-oz. pkg. instant chocolate
  pudding mix
2 c. milk

18-1/4 oz. pkg. chocolate cake
  mix
1 c. chocolate chips

Mix pudding with milk; blend until thick. Add cake mix; blend well.
Fold in chocolate chips; spread in a greased jelly-roll pan. Bake at
350 degrees for 25 to 30 minutes. Cool; cut into bars to serve. Makes
36 servings.

From-Scratch Brownies

Jane Davis
Newton, IA

Either frosted or left plain, they're delicious.

16-oz. can chocolate syrup
1/2 c. butter
1 c. all-purpose flour

1 c. sugar
4 eggs

Mix chocolate syrup, butter, flour and sugar together; add eggs,
one at a time, mixing well after each addition. Pour into a greased
13"x9" baking pan; bake at 350 degrees for 30 minutes. Makes 15 to
18 servings.

Reduce clutter in the bathroom...use pretty baskets to hold
everything from soaps, bath beads and lotions
to fluffy towels and washcloths.

Easy Vanilla Fudge

Connie Frey
Palmerton, PA

Stir in sweetened, dried cranberries for a touch of color.

8-oz. pkg. cream cheese,
  softened
4 c. powdered sugar

1-1/2 t. vanilla extract
12-oz. pkg. vanilla chips
3/4 c. chopped nuts

Blend cream cheese, powdered sugar and vanilla together until smooth and creamy; set aside. Melt chips in a double boiler; stir into cream cheese mixture, mixing well. Fold in nuts; pour into a lightly buttered 8"x8" baking pan. Refrigerate until firm; cut into squares to serve. Makes 4 dozen servings.

March mini evergreens up the stairs inside or out for extra winter festivity! Wrap the pots in burlap or homespun fabric and tie with holiday ribbon.

desserts

Rocky Road Bites

Ann Aiken
Spicewood, TX

It's hard to eat just one!

2 lbs. melting chocolate, melted
1 c. chopped pecans

10-1/2 oz. bag mini
   marshmallows

Mix ingredients together; spread on an aluminum foil-lined baking sheet. Let set for one hour; break into bite-size pieces. Makes 18 servings.

Easiest Pecan Pralines

Cindy Giles
Bossier City, LA

Made in the microwave...what could be easier?

1-lb. pkg. brown sugar
1/2 pt. whipping cream

2 T. margarine
2 c. pecan halves

Stir brown sugar and whipping cream together in a microwave-safe bowl; microwave in 2-minute intervals until sugar melts, stirring occasionally. Remove from microwave; stir in margarine and pecan halves. Drop by teaspoonfuls onto wax paper; set aside until firm. Makes about 3 dozen.

Look for vintage wrought iron trivets at antique shops and paint to match the kitchen. Hung on a wall or lined up on a shelf, they'll bring back memories of days gone by.

Winter

Mom's Best Popcorn Balls

Shari Miller
Hobart, IN

My mom made these for the holidays every year!

1/4 c. margarine
1/4 c. oil

10-oz. pkg. marshmallows,
  divided
4 qts. popped popcorn

Melt margarine in a heavy saucepan; add oil and half the bag of marshmallows, reserving the rest for use in another recipe. Stir until melted over medium heat; remove from heat. Place popcorn in a large roasting pan; pour marshmallow mixture on top. Stir until well coated; form into 3-inch balls using well-buttered hands. Wrap individually in plastic wrap. Makes 12 to 15.

Family Favorite Fudge

Brenda Kauffman
Harrisburg, PA

This creamy fudge recipe was given to my mother by my aunt back in the 1950's. My mother passed it onto me and now my family enjoys it just like I did as I was growing up.

1 c. butter
4 c. sugar
12-oz. can evaporated milk

12-oz. pkg. semi-sweet
  chocolate chips
13-oz. jar marshmallow creme

Combine butter, sugar and milk in a heavy saucepan; boil for 20 minutes, stirring often. Remove from heat; stir in chocolate chips and marshmallow creme until melted and smooth. Pour into a 13"x9" ungreased baking pan; set aside until firm. Cut into squares to serve. Makes 6 dozen.

desserts

Holiday Cookies

Laura Hagadorn
North Creek, NY

Not nuts about nuts? Use chopped, dried fruit instead!

1 c. butter, softened
3/4 c. sugar
2 c. all-purpose flour

1 c. walnuts, finely chopped
powdered sugar

Cream butter and sugar together; add flour, mixing well. Stir in walnuts; refrigerate for 30 minutes. Roll dough into one-inch balls; bake at 350 degrees on ungreased baking sheets for 12 minutes. Roll in powdered sugar while warm. Makes 2 dozen.

Make some edible gifts to pass out at this year's open house! Just cut out a star or a tree from a paper lunch bag, paste vellum over the hole from the inside to form a window...fill with homemade treats or candy and tie with bow!

White Chocolate Macaroons

Dottie McCraw
Oklahoma City, OK

Ready-made cookie dough makes these super simple.

18-oz. pkg. refrigerated white
   chocolate chunk cookie
   dough, thawed

2-1/4 c. flaked coconut
2 t. vanilla extract
1/2 t. coconut extract

Combine ingredients together; mix well. Drop by rounded teaspoonfuls onto ungreased baking sheets; bake at 350 degrees for 10 to 12 minutes. Cool on baking sheets for 2 minutes; remove to wire rack to cool to room temperature. Makes 24.

Create a fragrant Christmastime welcome by wrapping a few bunches of cinnamon sticks with holiday ribbon. Arrange them in a wicker basket with fresh, aromatic pine branches.

Index

Index

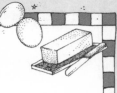

Index

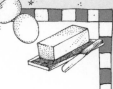

Index